KT-509-066

CRITICAL ACCLAIM FOR
:60 SECOND STRESS MANAGEMENT

'A perfectly wonderful book . . . has been praised
as the best written book on stress on the market'
Book Dealers World

'Goliszek discusses stress and its effects on the
body's ability to fight immunity. His book
addresses both the physical and mental
affects of stress and prescribes various relaxation
techniques and exercises . . . Well researched,
interesting and understandable'
Choice

'This guide to controlling stress, by research
scientist Goliszek, contains much useful
information for the lay reader . . .
A very useful book'
Library Journal

'Excellent . . . this is a text you can refer to over
and over. Your stress habits will be broken each
time you try one of the exercises. Keep it handy'
Guidepost

:60 SECOND STRESS MANAGEMENT
The Quickest Way To Relax and Ease Anxiety

Dr. Andrew Goliszek

BANTAM BOOKS

TORONTO • NEW YORK • LONDON • SYDNEY • AUCKLAND

:60 SECOND STRESS MANAGEMENT
A BANTAM BOOK : 0 553 40681 7

First publication in Great Britain

PRINTING HISTORY
Bantam Books edition published 1993

Bantam Books are published by Transworld Publishers Ltd,
61–63 Uxbridge Road, Ealing, London W5 5SA,
in Australia by Transworld Publishers (Australia) Pty Ltd,
15–25 Helles Avenue, Moorebank, NSW 2170,
and in New Zealand by Transworld Publishers (NZ) Ltd,
3 William Pickering Drive, Albany, Auckland.

Reproduced, printed and bound in Great Britain by
Cox & Wyman Ltd, Reading, Berks

Contents

Introduction

Abraham Lincoln once sat down and wrote:

"I am now the most miserable man living. If what I feel were equally distributed to the whole human family, there would be not one cheerful face on earth . . . I must die or be better."

It's been called the "Disease of the Twentieth Century," and it's believed to cause more ailments than anything else known to modern medicine. And, whether we realize it or not, for most of us it has become a habit we just can't seem to kick.

For years, doctors have been warning us that stress is harmful to our health; being exposed to it on a regular basis can trigger major problems such as cancer, hypertension, and coronary heart disease. Now, the latest evidence indicates that it could be a major factor in the jump from HIV infection to active AIDS.

So, with all the bad news about stress, why has it been so hard for us to break the stress habit and just learn to relax? The answer may be that we don't treat our stress responses with the same respect we treat any other habit. As a result, stress has become something we accept. We have learned to live—and die—with it. Changing our ingrained behavior takes time. But, it can be done.

How do you, as an individual, go about breaking the stress habit so that the quality of your life is better? First, by learning what stress is. Second, by learning to recognize your own stress symptoms. Third, by making changes in your behavior patterns. And fourth, by utilizing a series of quick and simple stress management relaxation techniques and exercises—":60 second stress managements"—that will effectively eliminate your own stress problems.

Every stress management exercise, technique and strategy should begin during those first sixty seconds.

":60 second stress managements" means simply that. Whatever relaxation techniques you employ, the decision to act during that first minute of stress is critical. You must condition yourself to become a ":60 second stress manager."

You'll soon discover that stress management has become a normal, but important, part of your life and realize that feeling good is really easy. It's never more than sixty seconds away.

· PART I ·

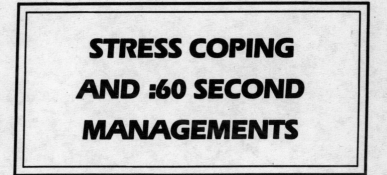

STRESS COPING
AND :60 SECOND
MANAGEMENTS

· Chapter 1 ·

Stress: What It Is and

What It Does

Harry comes home tired from work, still thinking about what he didn't complete that day. When he tries to have intercourse, he's still thinking about work and what he has to do the next day. Suddenly, he notices that he either cannot get an erection or cannot maintain one. Without realizing it, he blames his failure completely on himself. The next evening, he thinks about whether he will fail again. He tries harder and, because of his anxiety, fails again. The harder he tries, the more he fails. Soon, Harry begins to avoid intimacy and sexual contact altogether.

Harry is the victim of his own stress.

Our ancestors depended upon the stress response for life itself—to flee from predators, to fight enemies, and to survive in a hostile world. Those who were successful in responding to life-threatening events survived; those who couldn't, disappeared. Somewhere along the line, we developed into super-responders, able to react immediately to almost any life situation, yet unable to control the way we react. As a result, stress wove its way into every aspect of our society and became a part of our lives that we took for granted.

We respond to stress automatically—mostly out of habit—to thousands of events in our lives. Today, stress might be the result of having to deal with high-tech careers, fast paced business transactions, divorce, or social and family problems.

What began eons ago as a vital defense mechanism is today the leading cause of disease and illness in the modern world.

THE STRESS RESPONSE

You walk into your office Monday morning and see a stack of work. Something happens inside of you—you can sense it. If you're an overresponder, your body reacts with pain, nausea or anxiety. If you're a slow reactor, you may not get the message until you get home that evening, or after you've gone to bed.

But, overresponder or slow reactor, exactly the same things happen inside your body. No matter what is the source of stress or the time of reaction, the results are always the same. The person pressured by deadlines, the recent widow, the unprepared student or the patient who discovers he has a serious illness, all experience different stressors; yet all respond in the same biological manner. Our stress responses have evolved so that we don't have to worry about what to respond to and what to ignore; we respond to everything.

STRESS RESPONSE AS
A HABIT

A very common example of a stress-related response habit is male secondary impotence. Stress plays a major role in sexual problems because sexual activity is under the influence of the involuntary nervous system. Whenever a man gets aroused, nerve impulses from his brain cause blood vessels in the penis to dilate, allowing a flow of blood to enter the spongy tissue. At the same time, a sphincter muscle contracts and prevents blood from flowing back.

During any kind of stress, this muscle fails to contract and causes the penis to lose the blood needed for erection.

Here's a specific example:

John gets a new job and soon becomes irritated at some of the things his boss says to him. Since he needs the job, he can't do anything about it for fear of being fired. Every time he has a confrontation with his boss, John has a stress reaction. The reactions begin to come more easily, more quickly and of longer duration with each experience. Eventually, the mere anticipation of a confrontation will bring about a stress reaction. He experiences negative reactions at home, and on weekends, by just thinking about his boss. John's stress reaction has become a major habit and gets progressively worse and harder to break.

From the moment we're born, we become creatures of habit. We use our habits to free our minds of routine tasks and simplify our day-to-day existence. Habits are important. Performing simple tasks like writing, tying our shoes and eating with utensils are the direct result of habits. The problem occurs when we begin to acquire habits regardless of whether they're good or bad, positively or negatively reinforced.

Chronic stress response, then, is simply a bad habit that needs to be controlled. Our method of control will be a series of :60 second stress managements.

STRESS AND IMMUNITY

Immunity simply means having resistance to foreign particles or substances that enter the body. One theory of cancer growth suggests that everyone, at some point in their life, develops a cancer. The difference between those who fall victim to it and those who don't is a decreased immune response. Susceptible individuals may be the unlucky ones who become stressed more easily.

This correlation between the immune system and stress will become extremely important in our later discussion on the relationship between stress and AIDS.

STRESS-RELATED
ILLNESSES
AND DISEASES

A partial list of diseases believed to be partially blamed on long-term exposure to stress are coronary heart disease, hypertension, kidney disease, and arteriosclerosis. During the last decade, chronic backache, gastritis, migraine headaches, cold sores, hives, and ulcers also have been linked. The stress itself does not cause the illness but helps to bring it about by decreasing immunity.

Once we can discover the source of the stress and control it with a :60 second stress management, minor illnesses usually disappear.

How do we know it's stress causing many of our problems? In many parts of the world, where stress isn't a normal part of life, coronary heart disease is very rare. Once people in these areas are exposed to the stresses of modern society, they become as susceptible as anyone else. Other studies have shown that heart disease is linked to cholesterol levels which increase with stress. We know that smoking, obesity, alcohol consumption, kidney disorders, high salt intake, and heredity, can all raise blood pressure; but now we also know that stress can be a major factor in triggering the onset of hypertension.

In one study of nine- to sixteen-year-olds, it was discovered that a routine act such as reading out loud in front of classmates caused significant elevations in blood pressure. Studies continue to show that it's not only adults, but also children, who fall victim to hypertension as a direct result of stressful events in their lives.

Skins problems such as eczema, psoriasis, and shingles have been cured by using stress management techniques, since many skin diseases result from emotional stress.

Until recently, most illnesses were attributed to things like diet, heredity, environment, and lifestyle. Evidence now points in a new direction and links stress to a wide ranges of illnesses from headaches and ulcers to multiple sclerosis and cancer. Many of these illnesses and diseases can be controlled by learning to change attitudes and control thought patterns through simple :60 second management processes, which help keep our immune system from working overtime.

Managing stress is, without a doubt, one of the single most important elements in ensuring that defense is there and ready when it is needed the most!

Throughout the rest of this book, we will attempt to isolate particular stress problems and alleviate them with specific :60 second stress managements. By conditioning yourself to spontaneously relax, to relieve tension, to cope with conflict, and to eliminate anxiety, you'll gain freedom from stress and improve both the "quantity" and the "quality" of your life.

Chapter 2

Stress Signs, Symptoms and :60 Second Solutions

Bill starts having stomach pains when he goes to work. Instead of linking them with his job, he tries to discover what he has been eating that's making him ill. By automatically assuming that his stomach pain is caused by food, Bill is ignoring his body's cry for stress relief.

Joan begins to have back and neck pains during different parts of the day. She immediately assumes that the pains are being caused by the way she has been sleeping at night.

Both Bill and Joan are typical victims of stress without knowing it. They have not conditioned themselves to be aware of their bodies' stress signals.

The first step in relieving stress is to recognize certain symptoms that tell us our body is being stressed. Regardless of how stress affects us individually, it always leaves an unmistakable pattern of stress > symptom > illness. The trick is to recognize the symptom quickly and link it to the stress that it preceded. Being able to recognize certain stress-producing traits in our personality can help us to utilize quickly our :60 second stress managements to relieve stress symptoms.

RECOGNIZING STRESS SYMPTOMS

Not every reaction we have is a symptom of stress; we're all different. What may be a stress signal for one individual may be a sign of disease for another. Stress symptoms can be divided into three categories: physical, emotional and behavioral. Many of the symptoms listed below start out as minor irritants, but become progressively worse and may lead to serious stress-related diseases.

Physical Symptoms

- headaches

- twitching eyelid

- twitching nose

- facial or jaw pains

- dry mouth or throat

- difficulty in swallowing

- ulcers on tongue

- neck pains

- dizziness

- speech difficulties, slurring, or stuttering

- backaches

- muscle aches

- weakness

- constipation

- indigestion

- nausea and/or vomiting

- stomach pains

- diarrhea
- gain or loss of weight
- loss of appetite or constant appetite
- rashes, hives or other skin problems
- chest pains
- heartburn
- heart palpitations
- frequent urination
- cold hands and/or feet
- excessive sweating
- insomnia
- excessive sleeping
- sexual inadequacy
- high blood pressure
- chronic fatigue
- swollen joints
- increased allergies
- frequent colds and flu
- trembling and/or nervous tics
- accident proneness
- excessive menstruation or menstrual distress
- rapid or difficult breathing

Emotional Symptoms

- irritability
- moodiness
- depression
- unusual aggressiveness
- loss of memory or concentration
- restlessness or overexcitability
- nervous about little things
- nightmares
- impulsive behavior
- feelings of helplessness or frustration
- withdrawal from other people
- neurotic behavior
- racing thoughts or disorientation
- anger
- inability to make decisions
- anxiety
- feelings of panic
- frequent episodes of crying
- thoughts of suicide
- feelings of losing control

- lack of sexual interest

- periods of confusion

Behavioral Symptoms

- gnashing or grinding teeth

- wrinkling forehead

- high-pitched nervous laughter

- foot or finger tapping

- nail biting

- hair pulling or twirling

- increased smoking

- increased use of prescribed medication

- increased alcohol consumption

- compulsive eating

- compulsive dieting

- pacing the floor

- chronic procrastination

- loss of interest in physical appearance

- sudden change in social habits

- chronic tardiness

The reason we don't recognize minor stress symptoms is that we've become used to looking for the more common physical signals. Almost any kind of symptom can be a hidden signal of stress. Learning to recognize the small, insignificant signals can help us become more aware of our own sources of stress, prevent us from developing serious symptoms and make stress management easier.

LINKING STRESS SYMPTOMS TO STRESS SOURCES

One of the best ways to identify stress response patterns or hidden sources of stress is to keep a stress diary for at least two or three weeks.

The following is a sample of what your diary might look like—divided into four columns for Time of Day, Symptom, Immediate Activity and Previous Activity. Entries must be made as soon as noticed so that nothing gets forgotten or omitted.

As soon as we notice a stress symptom, we should write it down immediately, along with the time of day it occurs, the activity at the time and the thoughts we were having, and the activities and thoughts previous to the stress symptom. It is very important to include our thoughts, as well as physical activities, because thoughts can be potent triggers.

It is just as important to include previous activities and thoughts. Stress reactions do not always occur at the same time that stress occurs. To get a true indication, we need to train

Day/Date_____

Time of Day	Stress Symptom	Immediate Activity	Previous Activity
9:30 AM	Headache	Having breakfast Alone	Getting kids to school in a rush (9:00 AM)
12:30 PM	muscle Pain in neck & shoulders	Watching T.V.	Thinking about paying bills.
6:00 PM	Tapping foot constantly	Thinking about unpaid bills	Thinking about unpaid bills
10:00 PM	Stomach pain	Argument with Daughter	Watching T.V.
12:00 PM	Insomnia	Feeling Anger About Argument	Feeling Anger About Argument

ourselves to look back and remember what we have experienced during the past several hours.

After a week of keeping a stress diary, start looking for patterns. Do you usually get symptoms at a certain time of day? Do you get a specific symptom every time you do a certain thing or think a certain thought? Do you get sick an hour or more after you do something?

This is when we begin to play detective and look for clues that will lead us to our own hidden sources of stress. For example, we may notice that at 9:30 AM almost every day, we get a terrible headache. On closer inspection, we see that at 9:00 AM each day, we were busy rushing the kids off to school. On Monday, Tuesday, and Friday, we had trouble falling asleep. Our diary tells us that on those nights, we thought a lot about problems at work. At 7:00 PM on Wednesday and Thursday, we had diarrhea. According to our stress diary, at 5:30 PM on those nights, we were worried about having to go to weekly staff meetings while leaving the kids at home alone. Regardless of how insignificant our thoughts, feelings, or actions seem, we need to write them down. What might appear insignificant at the time could turn out to be a major trigger for stress symptoms.

Once we recognize our stress symptoms and link them to stress sources, the next step is to determine why the sources are causing the symptoms. We should ask ourselves these four questions:

1. Is the timing of the activity (time of day or night) causing stress symptoms?

2. Is the reason we're doing the activity causing stress symptoms?

3. Is the way we're doing the activity causing stress symptoms?

4. Is the amount of time spent doing the activity causing stress symptoms?

First, we need to assess whether or not it's the timing of whatever we're doing that's creating problems. Do the symptoms disappear when we change the time of activity? Is nighttime better than daytime? Does reorganizing our schedule make what we're doing less stressful? Next, we need to assess why we're doing what we're doing in the first place. Is it really necessary? Can we do without it? Next, we need to assess the manner in which we're doing what we're doing. Are we too intense? Do we worry the entire time? Do we use so much energy that we feel worn out? Finally, we need to assess how much time we spend doing what we're doing. Do we spend too much time? Do we spend too little time? Is the amount of time we spend interfering with more important things?

The answers to these questions tell us why the things we do, or the feelings we have, make us sick. Keeping an accurate stress diary will be physical proof that some of the little things we do, some of the little thoughts we have, are not so little after all! They need to be changed if we're serious about managing our stress.

At the end of our stress diary, we need to write down three things: (1) the exact cause of our stress symptoms (a physical activity, a thought, etc.); (2) the reason why the activity is causing the symptoms (timing, the way we do it, the reason for doing it, etc.); and (3) our goals for eliminating the stress symptoms. We can write something like this:

1. Cause of headaches: rushing to get the kids off to school every morning.

2. Reason for symptoms: timing—not enough time to do everything—feel rushed.

3. Solution: a) get up a little earlier

   b) organize my morning hours more efficiently

   c) don't leave things till the last minute

   d) prepare the night before

We should check our stress diary each day so we're sure of meeting at least some of our goals. As we accomplish one goal, we need to move on to the next until we eliminate stress symptoms altogether. Eventually, our natural ability to recognize stress symptoms will become easier. We'll be able to identify stress sources instantly.and act quickly before they become triggers for conditioned stress responses.

Even certain personality traits can be adjusted for our benefit if we recognize those traits as real sources of stress. "Type A" individuals, for example, are more prone to stress symptoms and stress reactions because they often don't link their symptoms with their normal behavior patterns. For them, keeping a stress diary is even more important than it is for the rest of us. But regardless of what type of personality type we are, we all need to realize that small and insignificant events can be major sources of stress and illness.

RECOGNIZING "TYPE A" VS. "TYPE B" BEHAVIOR

When heart disease became our nation's number one killer, it was thought that anyone leading a stressful lifestyle was at risk. It's now well-known that there's a certain behavior pattern called "Type A," which makes one more susceptible to coronary heart disease and other stress-related diseases because of specific character traits and mental attitudes. Many of these traits and attitudes are the reason for stress symptoms in the first place. Modifying Type A behavior patterns in order to relieve stress symptoms requires that we detect the traits in ourselves that make us either Type A or Type B individuals. We can then use stress management techniques to condition gradually ourselves to alter those traits.

Following are some differences between Type A individuals and Type B individuals. Not all Type A's and Type B's will have all or even most of these traits, but people typically fall into one or the other category.

Type A Characteristics

- Intensely competitive

- Impatient

- Achievement oriented

- Aggressive and driven

- Having a distorted sense of time urgency

- Moving rapidly and frequently

- Talking fast and listening impatiently

Type B Characteristics

- Relaxed and unhurried

- Patient

- Noncompetitive

- Nonaggressive

- Not having time urgency

In addition to these basic traits, Type A individuals have a greater cardiovascular response to stress, a greater increase in blood pressure, a greater release of adrenalin, higher blood chlesterol levels, and more extensive arteriosclerosis than Type B individuals. Type A individuals probably don't have all these problems at the same time, but normally they have enough of them to increase drastically their chances of becoming sick or diseased much sooner than Type B individuals.

TYPE A BEHAVIOR QUIZ

Many times, stress symptoms are the direct result of Type A behavior. Unless we become aware of our own Type A traits, recognizing stress symptoms and linking them to stress sources can be very difficult. The following quiz is designed to give you an idea of your own behavioral type. Read each statement carefully and then circle the number corresponding to the category of behavior that best fits you. (1 = Never; 2 = Seldom; 3 = sometimes; 4 = Usually; 5 = Always) When you finish, add up all the circled numbers. A key at the end of the quiz will explain what your total score means.

1. I become angry or irrita-
    ted whenever I have to
    stand in line for more than
    15 minutes.   1   2   3   4   ⑤

2. I handle more than one
   problem at a time.   1   2   3   (4) (5)

3. It's hard finding the time
   to relax and let myself go
   during the day.   1   2 (3) (4) 5

4. I become irritated or annoyed when someone is
   speaking too slowly.   1   2 (3) (4) 5

5. I try hard to win at sports
   or games.   1   2 (3) 4 (5)

6. When I lose at sports or
   games, I get angry at my-
   self or others.   1   2 (3) 4 (5)

7. I have trouble doing spe-
   cial things for myself.   (1) 2 (3) 4   5

8. I work much better under
   pressure or when meeting
   deadlines.   (1) 2   3   4 (5)

9. I find myself looking at my
   watch whenever I'm sitting around or not doing
   something active.   (1) 2 (3) 4   5

10. I bring work home with me.   1   2 (3) 4   5

11. I feel energized and exhil-
    arated after being in a
    pressure situation.   1   2 (3) (4) 5

12. I feel like I need to take
    charge of a group in order
    to get things moving.   1   2 (3) (4) 5

13. I find myself eating rap-
    idly in order to
    get back to work.   (1) (2) 3   4   5

14. I do things quickly regard-
    less of whether I have time
    or not.   1   2   3   (4)   5

15. I interrupt what people
    are saying when I think
    they're wrong.   1   (2)   3   4   5

16. I'm inflexible and rigid
    when it comes to changes
    at work or at home.   (1)   (2)   3   4   5

17. I become jittery and need
    to move whenever I'm try-
    ing to relax.   (1)   (2)   3   4   5

18. I find myself eating faster
    than the people I'm eating
    with.   (1)   2   (3)   4   5

19. At work, I need to perform
    more than one task at a
    time in order to feel pro-
    ductive.   (1)   2   (3)   4   (5)

20. I take less vacation time
    than I'm entitled to.   (1)   2   3   4   5

21. I find myself being very
    picky and looking at small
    details.   1   2   (3)   4   5

22. I become annoyed at peo-
    ple who don't work as
    hard as I do.   1   2   (3)   (4)   5

23. I find that there aren't
    enough things to do dur-
    ing the day.   (1)   (2)   3   4   5

24. I spend a good deal of my
    time thinking
    about my work.   1   2   3   (4)   (5)

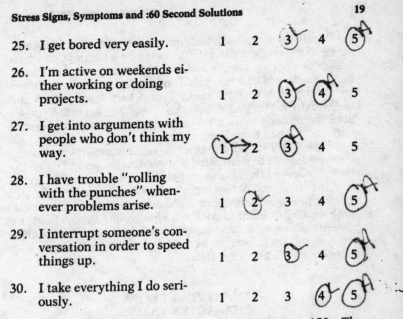

25. I get bored very easily.   1   2   ③   4   ⑤

26. I'm active on weekends either working or doing projects.   1   2   ③   ④   5

27. I get into arguments with people who don't think my way.   ①→2   ③   4   5

28. I have trouble "rolling with the punches" whenever problems arise.   1   ②   3   4   ⑤

29. I interrupt someone's conversation in order to speed things up.   1   2   ③   4   ⑤

30. I take everything I do seriously.   1   2   3   ④   ⑤

The minimum score is 30, the maximum 150. The breakdown by personality type is as follows:

SCORE	PERSONALITY TYPE
100-150	Type A 102
76-99	Type AB (Average) 81
30-75	Type B

If your score was 75 or below, you're a Type B person. You pretty much take life as it comes and usually don't allow problems and worries to dominate your life. If your score was in the range of 76 to 99, you're part of a majority who has some Type A and some Type B characteristics. For the most part, you probably know how to relax and aren't very aggressive or competitive. You do, however, take some things seriously and, in certain situations, like to be active, competitive, and productive. You need to see which Type A traits you have and decide whether or not they're affecting your health and lifestyle. If your score was 100 or above, then chances are you're a Type A person and you need to work on your attitudes, behavior, and priorities before you become seriously ill.

Because every person is different, there really are no absolute right or wrong answers. What may be a traumatic experience for one person may be a cakewalk for someone else. But no one, regardless of how energized and excited stress makes them feel, can keep up with too many Type A behavior patterns and stay healthy for very long. In fact, it's well known that Type A's suffer from many more kinds of stress symptoms and get sick much more often than Type B's do.

Type B or Type AB behavior is good because it allows us to achieve goals, to be motivated and productive, and to do all the things Type A's can do without being hostile, aggressive, impatient, or insecure. Achieving everything we want while still maintaining our composure and being able to relax is something we all can learn to do. By modifying our Type A behavior patterns and conditioning ourselves to adopt more Type B character traits, we'll become sick less often and make our lives more enjoyable and stress free.

MODIFYING TYPE A
CHARACTER TRAITS

We develop either Type A or Type B behavior as a result of our upbringing, our environment, and sometimes our genetic makeup. Therefore, modifying Type A behavior patterns in order to develop more Type B behavior patterns isn't achieved overnight. It takes practice and effort on our part and a sincere desire to want to change. But once we begin the process of adopting more Type B traits, it becomes easier and easier to conform because our brain will be trained to look at stressful situations in a completely different way.

The key to modifying Type A behavior is to break some of the long-term stress habits we've acquired. We do this by practicing special exercises that force us to acquire new habits at the same time we get rid of old habits. Many of us have Type A traits not because we're born with them but because we've repeated Type A behavior patterns so often they've become an unnatural part of our real personality. In essence, we've picked up some bad Type A habits. By actually practicing Type B behavior exercises, we'll gradually condition ourselves to eliminate some of our worst and most obvious Type A behavior traits. Once that happens, we'll be able to confront stressful situations knowing we can use our new Type B habits to combat stress and prevent its symptoms.

OVERCOMING STRESS-
RELATED TYPE A ANGER

Anger is the trait most responsible for the negative health effects of Type A behavior. The inability to control that anger can lead to premature heart attacks or other illnesses. Anger can be either the result of stress or a cause. Either way, it hinders our ability to function effectively and maintain a well-balanced and healthy life.

As we grow up, we learn to use anger in different ways. Some use it to get attention, others to get what they want, still others to vent feelings of frustration or aggression. In the past, experts have assured us that it was better to release anger than to keep it contained, but, as more studies have been done, it has become clearer that the most effective and healthy way to deal with anger is to prevent it originally or direct it into a more appropriate channel.

:60 SECOND STRESS
MANAGEMENTS FOR
ANGER

1. *Learn to be assertive.* Begin slowly if you feel uncomfortable, but take one minute per day to look for opportunities to communicate about minor issues so that you build up confidence to express feelings spontaneously and non-aggressively. (Making a list of these is helpful.)

2. *Identify the source of your anger.* Whenever you become angry, take sixty seconds to make sure you focus on the specific reason for that anger. Once you are focused, it will become easier to work on strategies that will eliminate the source of frustration.

3. *Use a third party to intervene.* Direct communication is not always possible. Take a minute to find and utilize a third party as a sounding board rather than close a matter entirely. Always try to resolve anger-causing conflicts as

22

:60 Second Stress Management

quickly as possible by working through someone you feel is willing, able, and qualified to assist.

4. *Try to be more understanding.* Try to become more aware of how the person with whom you are angry may be feeling. By nature, when we become more sympathetic, we have a tendency to be less aggressive and more accommodating. Take sixty seconds to define and consider the feelings of others and how those feelings may create even more anger for both of you.

5. *Find ways to prevent anger-causing situations.* Anger situations reoccur frequently. Identify the cause of your anger and find solutions to eliminate or bypass that cause. Anger actually can become intensified by repetition. Take sixty seconds to sit down with pencil and paper and diagram a method to eliminate the problem. This activity alone will relieve your angry feelings because you will be reacting positively to your anger.

:60 SECOND TYPE B BEHAVIOR EXERCISES

There are several practical exercises we can do to change our Type A habits and activities. After doing these exercises several times, they will eventually become automatic :60 second stress managements and even allow us to think up different ones using our own particular Type A behavior patterns. Practicing these exercises is important in habit formation because the physical act is a more powerful conditioner than just thinking about them. Conditioning, whether physical or mental, requires both mental and physical effort to achieve positive, lasting effects.

1. *Determine what activities arouse Type A behavior and reenact them utilizing Type B behavior.* Take sixty seconds to list them. For instance, if standing in line triggers stress symptoms, the next time you have to stand in a line try to consciously practice not being irritated or annoyed. Think about a pleasant upcoming weekend, a funny thing you read or saw on television, or a favorite experience. Thinking about pleasant things will eventually come easily and naturally.

2. *While eating, put your utensils down between bites.* Count to twenty. This will force you to slow your eating pattern and leave more time for conversation and interaction. Slowing down your eating habits will spill over into other activities, helping you to slow them down as well.

3. *Force yourself to do more recreational activities.* Take sixty seconds to make a list of things you might enjoy. For instance: Instead of reading job-related material, buy a book and enjoy it purely for the sake of reading. Make a date with yourself to go to a fun movie, take a joyous ride in the country or walk in the woods. In a short period of time, you will feel special and become aware of any negative behaviors affecting your health.

4. *Spend an entire day without your watch.* Make a real effort to forget time. A few periods without your watch will make you aware of how nice it is not to be a clock watcher.

5. *Pay attention to every frown and negative facial expression.* This exercise will train you to become acutely aware of the difference between negative and positive expressions. At the end of one day take 60 seconds to write down what you have noticed. After a week or two, any negative facial expression will instantly trigger an awareness. Being aware of negative expressions also will allow you to instantly recognize the sources of negative stress.

6. *Give yourself positive Type B self-instructions.* Take 60 seconds to make a list of Type B self-instructions. Don't be afraid to verbalize Type B expressions—relax, slow down, stay calm, don't rush, easy does it, etc.—out loud. Hearing them will add to their effectiveness. Eventually, they will become so automatic that you'll be able to retrieve them from your subconscious without having to verbalize at all.

7. *Reward yourself.* Take ten seconds to choose a Type B behavior pattern. Follow it for an entire week. At the end of a successful week, reward yourself with something special. Recognizing your accomplishment with a reward makes the conditioning process stronger.

At the end of our stress diary, we should have a section set aside for writing down our Type A character traits, our goals for modifying them into Type B character traits, and whether or not any of our stress symptoms are eliminated as a result of our changing from Type A to Type B. Here's how it might look:

Type A Traits	Type A Stress Symptoms	Goals for Modifying Type A Behavior	Symptoms Eliminated?
Impatient About waiting	1. Grinding teeth 2. Neck pains	Think positive & pleasant Thoughts when waiting in a line	1. YES 2. YES
Overscheduling work. Trying to do too much.	1. Headaches	Schedule only 1 thing at a time. Take periodic breaks.	1. YES
Always in a rush to go somewhere	1. Stomach pains 2. General muscle tension	Get up earlier. Do advance planning Organize time better	1. NO 2. YES

The idea behind practicing Type B character traits and keeping stress diary records is that once we recognize stress symptoms, become more aware of our behavior, and repeatedly perform constructive activities to modify that behavior, Type A stress management becomes a spontaneous one-minute mental exercise. That is, we eventually teach ourselves to "turn off" Type A character traits and "turn on" type B character traits in as little as one minute because our brain will be conditioned to guide our behavior in a Type B way. Again, this doesn't come easily at first. We've spent a lifetime acquiring Type A habits. But if we use the simple principle of habit formation by physically doing Type B activities, we can gradually eliminate almost any Type A habit. Having done this, we'll not only become healthier and happier, but we'll feel better about ourselves for having the strength to change our habits and for finally bringing out the Type B person that has been inside us all along.

· Chapter 3 ·

Good vs. Bad Stress

Recently, a group of lawyers were studied in relation to stress. It was discovered that the ones who became sick most often were the least stressed—exactly the opposite of what was expected! Delving further into the study, examiners found that the matter became clear when the manner in which lawyers were trained during law school was taken into consideration. For four years, they had been conditioned to believe that they performed better under pressure. When that pressure failed to materialize, they responded in just the opposite way from most of us.

The stress response is basically the same in all of us. The degree to which it affects us depends entirely on how we handle it. Getting into the habit of viewing stress as something constructive, rather than destructive, is the first step to becoming a more healthy and stress-free person.

STRESS TOLERANCE

We sometimes hear people say "I work better under pressure" or "I thrive on competition." These are individuals who automatically perform better when they're under the gun. Seemingly more satisfied when they are meeting deadlines, rushing to make sales, or doing anything that enhances the excitement of their lives, they are members of a minority for whom stress is not necessarily harmful and actually may be part and parcel of a healthy and productive life. For them, stress tolerance automatically takes negative situations and transforms them into positive events.

Our goal is to develop the kind of stress tolerance these people have without changing our personalities and without having to be pressured in order to feel good. Learning to do this is one of the critical elements in stress management.

One of the most popular theories about stress suggests that stress tolerant individuals possess an attitude of life with control, commitment, and a sense of purpose. Stress prone individuals, on the other hand, feel powerless about the events surrounding them. In general, we can say that good stress results from situations we can control, and bad stress results from situations over which we have no control.

Stress perception is influenced by many factors: age, intelligence, income, physical ability, level of education, religion, etc. For example, if we are expected to solve a difficult problem, we are naturally less stressed if we have the education and intelligence to solve the problem than if we don't. Likewise, if we are financially secure, our job security is not as stressful as it would be if we needed our job in order to support a family. In essence, the way we perceive stress is the critical factor in how we ultimately deal with it.

POSITIVE AND NEGATIVE
PERCEPTIONS

The first—and most important—mental reaction that occurs whenever we encounter any kind of situation or event is our perception of that event as either positive or negative.

A study done with nurses showed that those not involved in intensive care units experienced much higher levels of anxiety, reported more physical ailments and had greater work load dissatisfaction than those who were involved in high-stress positions. The indication was that intensive care nurses wanted (or needed) more challenge and felt more adventurous.

This and other studies demonstrate that certain individuals respond to stress in a positive way only because they are able to perceive stress events as challenging, rewarding experiences. This type of stress tolerance happens early during our

development and remains with us as a positive habit throughout life.

But, even if it doesn't, we still can have control over how
we respond to stress by using the power of our brain and our :60
second stress managements to change our perceptions. Once we
utilize these techniques, we can overcome our own natural
tendencies to be stress prone and join the ranks of the stress
tolerant.

STRESS TYPES

There are basically three types of individual: the type who
can't get along well without a stressful lifestyle; the type who
can't get along well without a quiet, peaceful life; and the type
who has the ability to get along perfectly with or without stress.
A certain amount of stress is essential for normal health, as long
as the amount doesn't exceed the coping ability of our own
personality. The danger comes when we mismatch our personality type and try to become something we're not. When that
happens, our normal personality becomes inhibited and we
either get too much or too little stress (usually too much).

Unfortunately, stress tolerance can be very deceptive, and
many individuals in high-stress careers make the mistake of
thinking that they as a group are stress tolerant. Careers don't
make people stress tolerant. If that were true, there wouldn't be
so many heart attack and ulcer victims among executives, doctors, air traffic controllers, and others in high-stress occupations. Individuals often try to be stress tolerant without first
developing a proper attitude or without using stress management techniques to help them boost their stress tolerance.
Thinking we're stress tolerant, regardless of occupation, is a
deadly mistake, especially if we've been subconsciously conditioned to be stress prone all along.

Knowing which personality type we are is important in
deciding our occupations, the kind of lifestyle we choose and
the kinds of activities we need to avoid. Before we can work
toward becoming stress tolerant, however, we need to examine
the type of personality we have in order to make the transition
from stress proneness to stress tolerance easier.

Unfortunately, most of us don't have the luxury of choosing

what our day-to-day experiences will be like. We go to work
and are forced to confront situations that lead to stress, anxiety,
and depression. Some of us feel helpless and alienated because
we can't or won't take control over the events in our lives. These
feelings intensify and eventually grow into major emotional
problems leading to ulcers, heart attacks, hypertension, and
many other stress-related illnesses. In order to prevent this
from happening, we need to develop a specific attitude called a
"stress-plus" or "stress tolerant" attitude. This kind of attitude
changes the way our brain interprets events and conditions us
to automatically or habitually turn negative situations into
positive experiences.

:60 SECOND STRESS
TOLERANT
MANAGEMENTS

Stress tolerance begins in the brain. It is there that we
must attack and change the conditioning process needed to
become stress tolerant. During this stage, there are five mental
images that must be present for stress to work for us instead of
against us. These mental images must be repeated until they
become part of our conscious day-to-day existence, part of our
unconscious behavior and ingrained as habits. Once they become part of our normal thinking process, they will become
automatic :60 second management switches, turning our stress
to a natural and positive response.

Mental Image #1. *I get a feeling of accomplishment and
strength whenever I'm committed or involved.*
    Whenever we become committed to a project, activity, or
job, we develop a sense of worth that's important in how we feel
about ourselves and what we're doing. Becoming actively involved and committed gives us purpose and direction. We begin
to lose the negative attitudes that stress brings on. Most of us
tend to be passive rather than active. By actively participating
and being involved and committed, we'll have a better outlook
on life and feel much better about ourselves in general. When
that happens, we'll automatically begin to experience more
positive and less negative events.

Mental Image #2. *I find change and/or challenge an exciting and rewarding experience.*

Too often we view changes in our lives as negative experiences. Even more often we allow changes to occur without making any effort at all to make positive experiences out of them. And sometimes we view change as neither positive nor negative and develop an attitude of complacency that causes us to have little if any feeling of excitement about anything. We always should be prepared to visualize the plus side of change rather than dwell on the minus side. Get in the habit of thinking about any change or challenge as exciting and rewarding. The more we do this, the less negatively we'll feel and the more excited we'll get.

A simple trick to use whenever we find that changing our routine is causing some anxiety is to do something special for ourselves at the start of each day. For example, we can begin the day by taking a walk, having a cup of tea and reading the paper, or sitting quietly and listening to our favorite program on the radio. Doing a little something extra for ourselves will make us feel special and give us the incentive to go out and meet those changes and challenges head on.

Mental Image #3. *I get a feeling of power that energizes me whenever I take control of situations.*

Having a feeling of control over events and situations is probably the most important and fundamental attitude we need in order to turn bad stress into good stress. We're discovering that bad stress isn't a result of job pressures and negative events but rather of the feelings we have that what we do is useless and that life is too complex and beyond our personal control. There's absolutely no way that we can receive any kind of positive feedback from a stress situation unless we feel like we have some kind of control over that situation. And if we feel in control, we have no problem channeling our energy into constructive activities.

One of the biggest problems we face as stress prone individuals is our inability to be in control of events that we should have been in control of all along. The more we begin to lose control, the more negatively we begin to feel and the more stressed we become. Eventually, every situation we encounter is one that we have little or no control over at all.

Having control is actually related to being involved and committed because involvement and commitment give us a sense of control and allow us to develop behavior patterns that automatically put us *in* control. Once we begin to feel like we're in charge of situations, we'll start meeting them head on instead of worrying about how they'll affect us. Soon, we'll realize that *controlling* is much easier and more rewarding for us than always *being* controlled.

Mental Image #4. *Stress brings out the qualities in me that make me most productive and worthwhile.*

Why would we willingly want to think that anything has the power to make us worthless and unproductive? Why should we deny ourselves the opportunity to be a better person just because we happen to be under pressure or stress? Imagine stress to be a battery that energizes us and without which we wouldn't be able to reach our full potential.

Good athletes know that, in order to perform well, they need intense competition and pressure. The great ones have developed the attitude that unless they're under pressure, they're just not going to be at their peak. This is why most world sporting records are set during the Olympics or during competitions when the best athletes are competing. These athletes actually believe that only the stress of competition brings out their best qualities. Their bodies respond to what their brain has been conditioned to perceive and, therefore, they need that extra pressure to stimulate themselves into making stress work for them. We need to become athletes in the sense that our performance and attitude always will be better when we're challenged. We'll quickly discover how effective stress can be in giving us the incentive to do our very best.

Mental Image #5. *I can transform any stressful situation into something positive.*

There's absolutely no reason why we can't think of something positive that will result from most stressful situations. When we can finally put this idea into practice, we'll have overcome the biggest obstacle in our becoming stress tolerant! The idea that we should be able to transform something negative into something positive is, in a way, a culmination of the first four mental attitudes. That is, if we become involved and committed, we'll begin to have a feeling of control over situations and make those situations exciting and rewarding experiences. Once that happens, we'll subconsciously and automatically believe that those same situations bring out the best in us and make us more productive and worthwhile. All these factors naturally will make us feel we can turn just about any negative event into a positive experience.

Integrating all these mental images into our own personality conditions us to make a conscientious effort to adopt a more positive attitude about stress. The attitude we choose determines whether or not we allow events to control us or whether we control them—and, consequently, whether or not we perceive stress as a challenge that we can overcome and mold to our own benefit. This small adjustment in the way we view challenges is the basic principle behind stress tolerance. By incorporating this simple principle into our daily lives, we can turn stress into a driving force that will enable us to perceive negative events in a very positive and constructive way.

:60 SECOND STRESS MANAGEMENTS FOR TURNING BAD STRESS INTO GOOD STRESS

The modification of our behavior patterns is primary to making it easier for us to change attitudes and make them fit our personalities. Changing some of our behavior patterns is critical to :60 second stress management and in developing stress tolerance. There are several basic methods of changing attitudes that will quickly lead to :60 second stress management techniques.

1. *Talk to yourself in a positive way.* Whenever we find ourselves in a stressful situation take a minute to find something positive in the event. The worst thing we can do is say something negative to ourselves.

2. *Visualize positive results.* It is common, when under stress, to visualize what we expect to happen. Stop and take :60 seconds to think about a good result—expect success—the outcome of a stressful situation will come naturally.

3. *Be flexible enough to change.* We shouldn't hesitate to change the way we approach problems. By being flexible, we may find a better method of accomplishing our goals and organizing our lives. We should have the wisdom and courage to do things a better way.

4. *Take time out.* Few of us can work for more than three or four hours without losing our ability to concentrate. We need a break every few hours to set our minds free and get back into a good frame of mind. Take a minute to schedule time for lunch, dinner or entertainment. Taking time for ourselves makes us feel we are important and gives us a sense of self-worth. When we make ourselves special, we automatically have a better outlook on life and improve our capacity to change our attitudes.

5. *Find the best work time and environment.* Most of us are either morning or night people. Determine your best time and plan as much as possible of your schedule around that time, doing your work at your peak energy levels.

6. *Exercise.* Exercise is one of the best ways to relieve tension and anxiety. It not only makes us feel energized and invigorated, but it also gives our immune system a boost. Exercise also releases endorphin, which not only suppresses pain but acts to give us a feeling of well-being and euphoria.

7. *Don't dwell on the past.* We can't do anything about the past, just the present and, perhaps, the future. Instead of worrying about what has happened in the past, we should take a minute to use past experiences in a positive way: "Okay, I didn't want to do it that way. I'll do it this way next time." Then, forget about it, and go on to more important things.

8. *Change or avoid the situation.* All of us have traits in our personalities that simply will not allow us to cope with

certain situations, even if we change our attitudes and behavior. When this happens, change or avoid the situation entirely. This may be hard to do, especially if it involves job or career, but most people will find that using all the :60 second stress management techniques available will help them improve their situations to the point of being able to cope with the most adverse conditions.

Turning negative events into positive experiences requires that we make adjustments in the way we think and in the way we act. Regardless of the kind of personality we have, conditioning ourselves to cope with stress through changes in our attitudes and behavior is the key element in developing a stress tolerant lifestyle.

All of us fall into certain personality molds that give us character amd make us unique individuals with different interests and varying behavior patterns. Somewhere within all of us, however, lies the ability to bring out the best in ourselves. We have the power to turn bad stress into good. How we perceive life events, how we behave in response to stress encounters, and how we condition ourselves to look at negative situations in a positive way all determine how quickly and easily we can begin to break the stress habit.

Chapter 4

Job Stress and Burnout

Bob became a teacher with the hope of making a real impact on children's lives. He graduated with the idea of being the best educator he could be. By his third year of teaching, Bob had begun to be frustrated at poor working conditions, a nonsupportive administration, angry and critical parents, and undisciplined students. Realities began to take their toll. Bob lost his enthusiasm, developed negative feelings, came to classes unprepared, and became detached from his students and fellow teachers. Eventually, the profession Bob loved so much was making him so ill that he chose to change careers.

The attitude that work is a duty and an obligation began with the early pioneers who settled this land. They believed that success and survival could be achieved only through cooperation, determination, and hard labor. This positive attitude toward work continued for generations, until a new and totally different society began to evolve. As our society developed, so did our concept of work. Instead of asking, "How will my work affect my neighbors?" we began to ask "How will I be affected by what I do?"

Gradually, work as a means of improving society was replaced by work as a means of enhancing our own status and standard of living. With the birth of the 'me' generation, work has become yet another source of stress. As job stress becomes such a routine part of our daily lives, relieving stress through changes in work habits, work environment, and work relations must be a key element in our overall stress managements.

SOURCES OF JOB STRESS

Just about any work situation can be a potential source of stress. The way we perceive our work situation will determine to what extent we're stressed and whether or not we'll experience serious stress symptoms.

In order to establish :60 second stress management procedures and handle job stress more effectively, we first must be able to recognize the things about our work that cause pressure. Following are ten of the most common job-related stress factors; many of us will have others beside those that are listed. Recognizing the ones that affect us personally is an important first step.

- Disorganization or inability to manage time

- Conflict with supervisors or colleagues

- Unqualified to do the job

- Feeling overwhelmed or overburdened by work

- Too much or too little responsibility

- Inability to meet deadlines

- Unable to adapt to changes in work routine

- Inability to utilize skills

- Feeling of boredom

- No support from superiors

Locked into a situation where we cannot make changes or decisions that will eliminate specific job stress factors, we must practice attitude and behavior modification exercises. We also should take time to learn relaxation techniques and time management strategies.

The first step, however, is to identify and write down anything about our work that leads to stress symptoms. We should handle this in exactly the same manner as our daily stress diary.

Think of job stress as just another stress. Remember, no matter what the stress, recognizing the symptoms, identifying the sources, and setting specific goals to eliminate and relieve the sources are the three important steps to establish :60 second management techniques.

EXPECTATION VS. REALITY

There's no such thing as a perfect job. Whatever career we choose, whatever job we do, there always will be the problem of altering or adjusting our expectations to meet reality. This often happens when we get our first job, when we change jobs, or when we get promoted. Our enthusiasm and eagerness for work quickly disappears when the reality of work and the problems associated with it begin to surface. Instead of being the exciting, rewarding occupation we expected, we see that, in reality, our job can be downright dull. Whenever our expectations exceed job reality but don't reach a balance after a certain period of time, we begin to experience the stress of "unattainable expectations." Here's an example of how some expectations and job realities can differ and become a real source of job stress.

EXPECTATION	REALITY
Work will be a challenging, stimulating, and rewarding experience.	Work is more often routine and sometimes very boring.
We'll be asked to use all our educational training or all our skills to do our job.	Much of what we learn in school is not practiced on the job. We often learn to do things the company way.
We'll be needed to utilize our abilities and intelligence in decision making and in implementing new ideas.	Decision making and the implementing of ideas are left to senior executives and managers.

These are only some of the ways expectations and job realities don't match up in the real world. The first thing we need to realize is that the standards we set for ourselves are sometimes too high, even for good companies to meet. Being reasonable in what we expect from our work will make our adjustment to reality much easier. If we're not, the stress of unattainable expectations can easily lead to deflated enthusiasm, cynicism, total job dissatisfaction, and burnout. These, in turn, can cause serious job-related illnesses such as ulcers, hypertension, and coronary heart disease.

When reality finally sets in, how do we cope with the fact that our expectations may never be realized? Instead of becoming depressed and isolated, we can begin to adjust to reality by accepting three irrefutable facts of work life:

1. Expectations in all areas of life, including work, are almost always distortions of reality. Reality, then, is always going to be a disappointment at first unless we accept the challenge and do something positive about it.

2. In almost all instances, work is something we need to fit into, not the other way around. No one is going to mold a job to meet our needs or demands unless we're someone very special. Positive attitudes make us more flexible and allow us to fit into almost any situation we want.

3. No job, regardless of what it is, is going to satisfy us unless we adopt attitudes and behaviors that condition us to perceive job events the way we want to perceive them. We can choose to make work either a pleasant or unpleasant experience through the power of our mind, and we can lower our expectations and still receive satisfaction from our work by setting realistic goals and by coming to terms with our negative feelings and attitudes.

Our job expectations, then, can be as powerful as our perceptions. If we expect something good to happen, and it doesn't, we naturally perceive our job situation in a negative way. If our expectations are so high that we never attain what we expect, then we begin to condition ourselves to perceive everything in a negative way all the time. We build subconscious images that reinforce and shape our attitudes and behavior, and we eventually form habits that strengthen our negative feelings toward work. The result is classic "burnout syndrome." Bringing expectations in line with reality can be difficult, but if we condition ourselves to perceive and accept job reality in a constructive way, we can avoid the pitfalls of chronic stress and burnout.

BURNOUT

The term "burnout" is often used these days whenever we talk about job stress because it has become a major problem in many professional and nonprofessional occupations. Burnout, simply put, is a gradual process by which a once productive and committed worker loses all concern and interest in his or her job or profession. Victims of burnout often experience physical and emotional exhaustion, total lack of interest in work, and detachment from fellow workers. Burnout isn't really the same as stress; rather, it's the direct result of prolonged exposure to stressful work conditions and situations.

Although burnout can strike anyone, the individuals most vulnerable are the ones who deal with people on a daily basis.

HIGH RISK
BURNOUT OCCUPATIONS

Although anyone in any profession can experience burnout, certain professions are especially vulnerable. These professions are health care, law enforcement, and teaching.

Many of the stress symptoms exhibited by different high risk groups are similar. Individuals in these groups should use any of the :60 second management strategies found throughout this book as a way of coping with stress and burnout. If you are not a member of any of these professions, you can still benefit from the suggestions and may well be able to identify with the problems experienced by high-risk individuals.

Physicians

The greatest source of emotional upheaval for physicians are therapeutic failures, diagnostic difficulties, death of young patients, and negative family impact. When these negative events become unbearable, some doctors may even contemplate suicide. Recent studies show that male physicians, as a group, are twice as suicide-prone as the general population.

For some physicians, it is difficult to deal with a dual standard between work and home environments. After being treated with awe and respect at work, for example, a physician may become angry and resentful when asked to take the garbage out or help do some laundry. This sudden drop in status can be difficult to conceive for individuals who are literally responsible for people's lives.

Physicians need to take immediate steps in order to keep from plunging deep into burnout. Some specific stress managements for physicians are:

1. *Reschedule time commitments.* Learn time management techniques.

2. *Schedule shorter rotations during intense work conditions.*

3. *Increase vacation time and time away from work.*

4. *Vary daily routines.*

5. *Become involved in outside activities and organizations.*

6. *Exercise.*

7. *Seek out support networks with other physicians.*

Nurses

Nurses also experience burnout—but for different reasons. They have to deal not only with demanding patients but with stressed-out physicians as well. This dual source of stress is often the reason why nurses feel overburdened, overworked, and underappreciated.

Young nurses begin their careers with unusual enthusiasm and idealism, believing that nursing is a very special profession. When they begin to encounter critical, demanding, and ungrateful patients or physicians who treat them like second class citizens, their idealism is shattered. One of the biggest reasons for rapid burnout in nurses is this disparity between expectation and reality

Quick solutions are necessary to ease burnout. One study showed that nurses practicing relaxation techniques for as little as twenty minutes a day had a much better ability to cope with stress, had a marked improvement in anxiety levels, increased their work energy, and had greater job satisfaction than those who didn't. Specific stress techniques nurses can use are:

1. *Adjust work schedules.* Temper the care of dying or critically ill patients with others.

2. *Get involved in outside activities or volunteer work unrelated to health care.*

3. *Take time off to go on trips or just to relax.*

4. *Exercise.*

5. *Maintain regular sleep patterns.*

Police Officers

A recent survey found that 10 percent of all "heavy drinkers" were police officers and that a high percentage of all police officers admitted to having a drink while on duty. Furthermore, it was found that alcohol-related cirrhosis of the liver was significantly higher among police officers than among the population in general. One of the biggest reasons for this high alcohol use, it was discovered, was the feeling by police officers that they had no control over their work. And since most police organizations are militaristic and require discipline and strict adherance to regulations, police officers often turn to alcohol as an outlet to vent their frustrations and to cope with the stress of their career.

Stress-related disorders among police officers include various physical disorders, emotional and personal problems, and impaired work performance. Physical disorders range from backaches, muscle cramps, and headaches to asthma, high blood pressure, heartburn, and ulcers. Studies also have found high rates of coronary heart disease and digestive disorders. Emotional and personal problems include divorce, alcoholism, depression, and suicide.

The very nature of police business, which often emphasizes authoritarianism and depersonalization, can cause police officers to feel isolated and lonely. This, in turn, can easily lead to aggressive behavior, apathy, cynicism, disobedience to regulations, and withdrawal from the public and fellow workers.

Some specific stress relaxation techniques for police officers are:

1. *Develop or find a social support group that includes other police officers.*

2. *Take time off from police work completely.*

3. *Seek counseling in serious cases.*

4. *Do volunteer work within the community.*

This last strategy is a key element in eliminating hostility and suspicion toward police officers within their own communities. Since hostility and suspicion often are responsible for creating the isolation, withdrawal, and loneliness that leads to police burnout, getting involved in the community can be a great way to cope.

Teachers

When we hear the word burnout, many of us immediately think of the teaching profession. Teacher burnout is critical because it directly affects our children; and whether it happens in kindergarten or high school, teacher burnout affects the attitudes children have toward school and, more importantly, the enthusiasm they have about learning. If it occurs in the lower grades, it causes children to develop negative feelings about the entire school experience. If it occurs in the upper grades, it creates an apathetic and tense atmosphere in which older children are stifled at a time in their lives when the learning process can become especially vulnerable to negative reinforcement. But regardless of when it occurs, teacher burnout will invariably affect children by causing intensely negative feelings about education in general.

As with other professions in which burnout is common, teachers encounter the same problem of expectation versus reality. Young teachers graduate from college ready to be the best educators they can be and wanting to make a life-long impact on children's lives. And because of their idealism, they often blame themselves for not being able to improve a system they see as failing its students. Instead of realizing their expectations, teachers quickly encounter the realities of teaching, lose their enthusiasm for work, experience job dissatisfaction, and end up feeling cynical and frustrated.

Comprehensive burnout management for teachers requires goals that put things back into perspective so that the reality of the classroom is approached in a positive way.

Some specific stress relaxation techniques for teachers are:

1. *Continue to improve work skills.* Taking classes, attending seminars and participating in extra job training will prevent feelings of inadequacy.

2. *Schedule "down time."* Coffee breaks and lunches shouldn't be used for grading papers or reading reports. Teachers need time away from school duties.

3. *Keep abreast of new ideas.* Using the same class notes and materials year after year will invariably lead to boredom and burnout. By updating lesson plans and notes, teachers can stay interested in teaching.

4. *Form teacher support groups.* Communicate with and exchange ideas with fellow workers.

5. *Become a time management expert.* A great deal of teaching burnout results from an inability to manage time effectively. As projects grow too large to handle and responsibilities become overwhelming, teachers need to put time management strategies into practice.

Not only workers in these specific categories need to be especially wary of symptoms that indicate early warnings of burnout syndrome. Other jobs that promote burnout are ones in which workers do repetitive or routine tasks, do not receive positive feedback, or have great responsibility but little control. Some of the types of individuals most susceptible to burnout syndrome are perfectionists, egotists, idealists and workaholics.

BURNOUT RATING QUIZ

The following quiz is one way to rate how prone we are to burnout, or our "burnout index." Following the quiz is a scoring key and a list containing some common signs and symptoms that are associated with burnout or that are seen shortly prior to burnout.

		Seldom	Some-times	Always
1.	I feel hostile or angry at work.	1	2	3
2.	I feel like I have to succeed all the time.	1	2	3
3.	I find myself withdrawing from co-workers.	1	2	3
4.	I feel like everything I'm asked to do is an imposition.	1	2	3
5.	I find myself increasingly insensitive or callous to clients, co-workers, or associates.	1	2	3
6.	Work has become very boring, tedious, and routine.	1	2	3
7.	I feel like I'm at a standstill in my career.	1	2	3
8.	I find myself feeling negative about work and focusing only on its bad aspects.	1	2	3
9.	I find myself accomplishing less than I ever have before.	1	2	3

		Seldom	Some-times	Always
10.	I have trouble organizing my work and my time.	1	2	3
11.	I'm more short-tempered than I've ever been before.	1	2	3
12.	I feel inadequate and powerless to make changes at work.	1	2	3
13.	I find myself taking out my work frustrations at home.	1	2	3
14.	I consciously avoid personal contact more than I ever have.	1	2	3
15.	I find myself asking whether my job is right for me.	1	2	3
16.	I find myself thinking negatively about work even when I go to bed at night.	1	2	3
17.	I approach each work day with the attitude of "I don't know if I'm going to make it through another day."	1	2	3
18.	I feel as if no one at work cares about what I do.	1	2	3
19.	I find myself spending less time working and more time avoiding work.	1	2	3

	Seldom	Some-times	Always
20. I feel tired or exhausted at work even when I get enough sleep at night.	1	2	3

Scoring Key: 20-34
No Burnout

35-49
Moderate Burnout (early warning signs)

50-60
Severe Burnout (need help & guidance)

SIGNS AND SYMPTOMS OF BURNOUT

Absenteeism	Hostility
Alcoholism	Indifference
Anxiety	Insensitivity
Apathy	Irritability
Boredom	Isolation
Callousness	Job dissatisfaction
Conflicts with workers	Low morale
Cynicism	Malaise
Defensiveness	Marital problems
Disillusionment	Moodiness
Depersonalization	Negativism
Depression	Paranoia
Drug dependence	Pessimism
Exhaustion	Reduced accomplishments
Family problems	Resentment
Fatigue	Sexual problems
Fault finding	Suicide thoughts
Frustration	Weakness
Hopelessness	Withdrawal

If we're on the road to burnout, we'll probably experience several of these symptoms before the final stage of burnout occurs. But no matter what the cause is, burnout always involves a pattern that leaves us de-energized and emotionally exhausted.

Burnout is essentially the result of "unrelieved job stress." Whenever we feel trapped in our job or helpless to solve problems or conflicts, the reality of our helplessness causes frustration, anxiety and a feeling of powerlessness. This frustration is transmitted to the people we work with and results in a work environment that becomes unbearable and depersonalized.

Nancy was a young nurse who graduated near the top of her class. She brought with her an enthusiastic desire to help her patients and was eager to do everything she could to become an ideal nurse. After all, as a youngster, Nancy was given a glamorous and idealistic picture of nursing, and she continued to have that picture in her mind while in school. Shortly after she began work, however, she encountered critical and ungrateful patients and physicians who treated her like a second class citizen. Her expectation of what nursing was really like was shattered. Gradually, Nancy began to develop negative attitudes about patients and doctors, became hostile and short-tempered, and started to withdraw from her co-workers. In the end, Nancy became so bitter, cynical, angry, and dissatisfied that she was a threat to her patients.

There are four stages of burnout syndrome. We need to be aware of each stage in order to recognize the warning signals that tell us there's danger ahead.

Nancy went through the four stages of burnout before she finally burned herself out completely. Had she caught the burnout during the first three stages, she could have reversed the process and become a happy, productive worker again. Very few individuals, however, can reverse the burnout process entirely once they've remained in the fourth and final stage of burnout for any length of time.

FOUR STAGES OF
BURNOUT SYNDROME

Stage 1. High Expectations and Idealism

Symptoms: Enthusiasm about the job
Dedication and commitment to work
High energy levels and accomplishments
Positive and constructive attitudes
Good outlook

Stage 2.   Pessimism and Early Job Dissatisfaction

Symptoms: Physical and mental fatigue
Frustration and disillusionment
Lowered morale
Boredom
Early stress symptoms

Stage 3.   Withdrawal and Isolation

Symptoms: Avoiding contact with co-workers
Anger and hostility
Severe negativism
Depression and other emotional distress
Inability to think or concentrate
Extreme physical and mental fatigue
Excessive amounts of stress symptoms

Stage 4.   Irreversible Detachment and Loss of Interest

Symptoms: Very low self-esteem
Chronic absenteeism
Terminally negative feelings about work
Total cynicism
Inability to interact with others
Serious emotional distress
Severe physical and emotional stress symptoms

ELEVEN :60 SECOND BURNOUT "EXTINGUISHERS"

Unless we've gone into the fourth and final stage of burnout, we can reverse the process through simple changes in our job goals, attitudes and behaviors. Here are some very effective coping strategies—proven burnout "extinguishers"—that will lead to :60 second management techniques:

1. *Express feelings and emotions.* Putting stress into words through communication with colleagues can prevent the isolation often felt during the later stages of burnout. The exchange of ideas acts as a buffer because sharing and communicating has a unique way of relieving stress and putting things in perspective.

2. *Schedule down time.* Everyone needs breaks away from work. Instead of using lunch or coffee breaks to catch up on unfinished or extra work, spend down time doing something completely unrelated to work. Time off is absolutely essential in refreshing attitudes and job outlook.

3. *Recognize energy patterns and schedule work accordingly.* During a normal work day, we all have high and low levels of energy. Finding out when high energy levels occur and then scheduling stressful duties only during those times will prevent wear out and energy loss.

4. *Never schedule more than one stressful activity at the same time.* This may take some thought and planning beforehand, but putting up with only one stressful situation at any given time will prevent work pileup, make you feel like you're accomplishing more, and relieve the stress of feeling overworked.

5. *Engage in outside physical activities.* It's very important to participate in physical exercise because stimulating the body refreshes the mind. Our brain requires activity by the rest of our body in order to revitalize the senses and enhance performance. Exercise also builds physical resistance and makes us feel better about ourselves. When stagnation sets in, resistance and energy are lowered, and the natural tendency is to become more susceptible to physical and emotional distress.

6. *Break projects down into smaller parts.* Some of us have a tendency to become overwhelmed by a project soon after we start it. By cutting a big project down to its individual components, it never looks as difficult or overwhelming. We can then tackle it piece by piece and never even realize how big it is until it's finally done.

7. *Delegate responsibility.* If we're ever in a position to delegate responsibility to others, we should make it a point to do so. Rather than take on every problem that comes up, we need to allow others to share in problem solving and decision making.

8. *Learn to say no.* Never feel obligated to take on extra assignments or do special projects which aren't required but which cause feelings of anger and hostility. Saying yes all the time makes us feel helpless, while being able to say no gives us a feeling of control and satisfaction. This isn't the same as not wanting to get involved and committed. Giving ourselves the choice of what we want to be involved in or committed to is the kind of control we need to have to become stress-free.

9. *Improve work skills.* We need to become more aware of new changes and keep abreast of current technologies and ideas. Taking classes, going to seminars and participating in extra job training will keep us up-to-date and prevent feelings of inadequacy. If we don't we'll become more and more withdrawn and isolated. Eventually, our inability to work effectively with others will cause serious emotional problems.

10. *Strive for success.* Never be satisfied with doing only what you've been trained to do. Successful individuals learn new things, take risks, go out of their way to improve career goals, and are anxious to meet new and exciting challenges. If you're willing to extend yourself and reach for success, then chances are you'll never experience burnout.

11. *Learn to relax.* Set aside some time each day to bring your body back to a state of "relaxed equilibrium." Learning the art of conscious relaxation (discussed in a later chapter) will have a greater benefit than sleep and allow you to accept and cope with stressful situations more readily.

Two myths about burnout are that it occurs suddenly and that it only happens to workers in certain occupations. In reality, burnout can happen to anyone. It usually develops slowly and can take years before the symptoms of burnout manifest themselves as physical and emotional problems.

The good news is that it's easily recognizable and easily reversible during the first several stages. Dealing with burnout, however, requires both preventive action and stress reduction. Practicing the coping strategies discussed in this chapter attacks the root of job stress and job dissatisfaction caused by attitudes and behaviors. Using the relaxation techniques discussed in later chapters, together with these coping strategies, will make it easier to reverse the burnout process and help you experience a fuller and more rewarding work life.

• Chapter 5 •

Time Management

One of the biggest stress factors we face, whether it's at work or at home, is our inability to manage time. Time management, or the lack of it, creates stress because without time we loose the freedom to do what needs to be done, to be who we want to be, and to enjoy the things we want to do. We accomplish only what we can "fit into our schedules." And we find ourselves pressured because our lives and our work are constantly dictated by time.

Time management, then, allows us to organize our lives in a way that makes us happier and more productive; it gives us the ability to schedule ourselves into a normal day-to-day routine so we're left with the time we need for ourselves and our family; and it prevents chronic stress by eliminating the constraints we place on ourselves as a result of poor or inadequate organizational skills.

The following time quiz should help identify trouble spots and guide us toward our goal of becoming successful time managers. Read each statement carefully and circle the corresponding number that comes "closest" to answering the statement. (1 = Always; 2 = Usually; 3 = Sometimes; 4 = Rarely) At the end of the quiz is a scoring key which indicates levels of time management skills.

1. I find that I have enough
    time for myself—to do the
    things I enjoy doing.   .   1   2   3   4

2. I'm aware of deadlines and schedule my work to meet them in plenty of time.

    1   2   3   4

3. I write down specific objectives in order to work toward goals.

    1   2   3   4

4. I use a calendar to write down appointments, deadlines, things to do, general notes.

    1   2   3   4

5. I feel in control of time while at work and at home.

    1   2   3   4

6. I plan and schedule my time on a weekly and/or monthly basis.

    1   2   3   4

7. I make a daily to-do list and refer to it several times per day.

    1   2   3   4

8. I set priorities in order of importance and then schedule time around them.

    1   2   3   4

9. I'm able to find blocks of time when I need them in case something important or extra has to be fit in.

    1   2   3   4

10. I'm able to say no when I'm pressed for time.

    1   2   3   4

11. I try to delegate responsibility to others in order to make more time for myself.

    1   2   3   4

12. I organize my desk and work area to prevent clutter and confusion.

    1   2   3   4

13. I find it easy to eliminate or reschedule low priority items.

    1   2   3   4

14. I try to do things in a way that cuts down on duplicated effort.

    1   2   3   4

15. I find that doing everything myself is very inefficient.

    1   2   3   4

16. I try to shift priorities as soon as they change.

    1   2   3   4

17. I find it easy to identify sources of time problems.

    1   2   3   4

18. I find it easy to eliminate or reshuffle unnecessary paperwork.

    1   2   3   4

19. My meetings and activities are well organized and efficient.

    1   2   3   4

20. I know what I'm capable of and try not to overextend myself.

    1   2   3   4

21. I find it easy to keep up with changes that affect my schedule or workload.

    1   2   3   4

22. I know what my responsibilities and duties are.

    1   2   3   4

23. I try to schedule the most difficult work during my most productive times.

    1   2   3   4

24. I try to get only the pertinent information before making a decision rather

than trying to get as much information as possible.	1 2	3	4

25. I finish one job or task be-
fore going on to the next.   1   2   3   4

Scoring key: 25- 40≑Excellent time manager
                41- 55≑Good time manager
                56-100≑Poor time manager

After completing the quiz, we need to go back and identify those areas that are the most consistent sources of time-related stress. By recognizing the specific behavior patterns and attitudes that interfere with our ability to organize, manage, and schedule time, we can begin to reverse time management problems quickly and effectively. The most common areas to look for are:

- Not prioritizing tasks

- Not scheduling daily, weekly, or monthly activities

- Not delegating responsibility

- Not being able to say no

- Not writing down objectives in order to meet deadlines

- Not using a calendar to organize commitments

- Not shifting priorities to make room for more urgent tasks

- Not reducing clutter and unnecessary paperwork

- Not being able to give up total control

- Not being able to avoid procrastination

These are only the most common areas of poor time management. We all have our own individual weaknesses and, therefore, we need to recognize and eliminate those weaknesses by writing them down in a time management diary. The four areas that should be included in our diary are:

1. The event or activity.

2. Its priority ranking.
   1 = important
   2 = less important
   3 = least important
   4 = not important at all

3. The action we take.

4. A strategy for improving the way we handle the event or activity in order to enhance time management skills.

TIME MANAGEMENT DIARY

A week of writing down activities and actions should be enough to indicate where time problems lie and what sorts of strategies we can take to eliminate wasted effort. At the end of each day, write down "specific timewasters" and make a list of strategies that will solve problems dealing with those timewasters. Here's an example:

Keeping a diary of activities and an accurate record of timewasters should give us a clear picture of how we're doing as time managers and how far we need to go to become ideal time managers. It's impossible to practice time management without first knowing what it is that makes us so poor at accomplishing a certain amount of work in a given amount of time. Once we put our finger on the problems and their sources, we can begin to adjust our daily behavior patterns in order to eliminate the root of our time-related stress. This is where conditioning and habit formation come into play once again. By consciously practicing good time management activities, we'll begin to break our old time management habits and condition ourselves to develop new and more effective behavior patterns.

Time Management Diary

Time	Activity	Priority Ranking	Action Taken	Improvement Strategy
7:00				
7:30				
8:00				
8:30				
9:00				
9:30				
10:00				
10:30				
11:00				
11:30				
12:00				
12:30				
1:00				
1:30				

FIFTEEN :60 SECOND
TIME MANAGEMENT
STRATEGIES

The recurring theme of conditioning and habit formation is a powerful force in shaping our :60 second management techniques. Time management is no different. The positive re-

2:00				
2:30				
3:00				
3:30				
4:00				
4:30				
5:00				
5:30				
6:00				
6:30				
7:00				
7:30				
8:00				
8:30				
9:00				
9:30				
10:00				

inforcer of good time management is a rewarding and satisfying experience. The more effectively we manage our time, the less stress we will feel and the more positive the conditioning process becomes. Eventually, good time management will become a permanent and natural :60 second reaction to stress:

Nothing comes easily at first: Our habits will prevent us

Timewaster	Strategy
Looking through every piece of mail.	Discard junk mail immediately. Put low priority mail aside until more time is available.
Having meetings that go on for a long time.	Make a meeting agenda and don't go beyond a specific time limit. Prepare better.
Having a lot of small duties that interfere with more important tasks.	Prioritize duties and/or delegate some of the lesser responsibilities to others. Eliminate unnecessary tasks.

from becoming ideal time managers overnight. Only through repetition can we shape our behavior in the manner we choose. Here are fifteen ways to develop good time management habits and achieve our number one goal of automatic :60 second management stress relaxation techniques:

1. *Write down weekly goals, plans, activities and objectives.* This kind of a tentative to-do list will get the wheels rolling and make further planning and scheduling easier.

2. *Prioritize tasks according to importance.* After writing down these activities, give them a priority ranking: top, high, low or least.

3. *Plan schedules in an organized manner by using a calendar or appointment book.* These tools are organized in a way that makes scheduling and planning easy, effective, and manageable.

4. *Schedule demanding tasks during periods of high energy.* There are morning, noon, and night people. Scheduling in this manner will allow you to do your best on the most important assignments.

5. *Eliminate timewasting activities.* Eliminate all the things you do every day that are unnecessary. Put them at the end of the list.

6. *Delegate authority.* One of the biggest causes of stress comes from the attitude that you have to do it all yourself. Take a look at your schedule and decide what can be handled by someone else.

7. *Finish one task before starting another.* Some of us can handle several things at the same time; most of us can't. Assign a priority rating to each task and eliminate the tendency to procrastinate.

8. *Write it down.* Taking good notes supplies you with information, reminds you of priorities and provides you with a backup to your calendar. Always keep a pencil and small note pad available and get in the habit of using it.

9. *Learn to say no.* Of all time management techniques, learning to say no is one of the best :60 second ways to avoid scheduling problems, eliminate timewasting activities and stay in control of day-to-day planning.

10. *Leave some of your schedule open.* Never fill up your schedule completely. By leaving yourself available time for emergency meetings or unexpected jobs, you'll be less anxious about your ability to schedule "just one more thing."

11. *Develop and keep deadlines.* Don't put off projects. Procrastination just makes deadlines harder to meet. Know when your deadlines are and keep them.

12. *Don't put off making decisions.* Effective decision making doesn't necessarily mean waiting until you have every fact and figure. Write down the decision you have to make, list the primary facts and figures that you need, get them as quickly as possible, and make your decision.

13. *Improve reading and writing skills.* Effective communication, including the ability to read quickly and write coherently, is basic to all effective time management.

14. *Develop an effective reminder system.* No one can remember everything. Without a reminder, follow-up material and attention to small details suffer.

15. *Be in control.* Being in control is as important in time management as in stress management. In any time management situation, the telephone can be your worst enemy. Avoid unnecessary calls or long conversations. If at all possible, avoid answering your own phone. Avoid unnecessary socializing. Avoid getting involved in events not concerned with your job. Avoid unorganized meetings or discussions.

It's not the things we do during the day that create time problems, it's the way we do them. More often than not, the reasons for our inability to manage time are improper behavior patterns and attitudes. Behavior and attitudes can both be changed through proper techniques and conditioning. Both can be used as positive reinforcers that make us more efficient at utilizing the time we have. As a first step, however, we need to recognize those things about ourselves that cause time-related stress.

· Chapter 6 ·

Stress and Mental Health

Throughout history, mental health problems have been depicted in stories about people being "possessed by demons" and acting in an "ungodly and unnatural way." The stigma of being different was so great that mental health was largely ignored or hidden for much of our history. But with increased modernization came increasing anxiety, depression, and psychoses, and we began to look more closely at mental health disorders. We learned that mental illnesses were linked to the stresses we ourselves had created. Stress is now regarded as one of the main causes of mental and emotional problems.

The reasons individuals develop mental health disorders are complex, and it would be simplistic to attribute all mental health problems to stress alone. But mental health and stability can be affected deeply by the way we handle stress; certain coping strategies are vital in relieving the emotional traumas and mental disorders caused directly by prolonged exposure to stress.

DEPRESSION

Psychiatrists consider many kinds of depression to be a response to emotional stress rather than a specific disease or illness. Treatment by many doctors is through individual coping strategies and various stress management techniques. We all become depressed at one time or another, and we all exhibit different signs and symbols of depression. Depression can be something as simple as sadness, or something as severe as deep withdrawal. Here is a list of common symptoms that can be used as a guide to recognizing certain traits and behaviors of depression:

- Insomnia or excessive sleep

- Compulsive behavior (overeating, anorexia, bulimia, etc.)

- Withdrawal and isolation

- Loss of control

- Loss of memory and/or concentration

- Disinterest in work or other activities

- Physical pains (headaches, backaches, etc.)

- Feelings of loneliness and/or emptiness

- Frequent self-doubts and self-criticism

- Irritability

- Excessive alcohol or drug abuse

- Loss of interest in sex

- Thoughts of or attempts at suicide

- Enduring feelings of sadness, guilt, or hopelessness

When we look at specific examples of mental health problems, we discover that stressful negative life events account for a large number of depression cases. Many studies have clearly demonstrated that depressed individuals experience stressful life events in the months that precede the start of their depression.

But, in many cases, the stress events that cause depression are small, repetitive occurrences rather than major stress events. The cumulative effect can be equally, if not more, potent than major ones because of their frequency.

But, if there's one positive side to depression, it's that, in almost every case, it's easy to recognize. Early warning signals allow us to deal with our stress immediately and effectively before depression slips into a dangerous and chronic stage.

FOUR :60 SECOND
STRESS MANAGEMENTS
FOR DEPRESSION

Unless depression is severe and caused by deep emotional problems, certain coping strategies can be used to reverse or lessen depression syndrome. Here are four main coping techniques that will lead to :60 second managements for depression:

1. *Increase social contacts and interactions with friends and family*. Take :60 seconds to make a list of people you enjoy being with. Make an effort to broaden your circle of friends and see them on a regular basis. Stress and depression decrease as interactions increase.

2. *Improve communications between yourself and others*. This is especially true of verbal communication between family members. Communication opens doors and makes relationships grow. Take :60 seconds to really "listen" to the person with whom you're speaking.

3. *Develop social support systems*. Social support systems may include a group of friends, your community, your church, or your family. This one strategy can greatly brighten your outlook on life.

4. *Become involved*. Taking part in activities, events, organizations and social groups will get your mind off the source of stress. Many depressed individuals discover that involvement alone is not only the answer to their stress, but many of their mental problems.

The best treatment for depression really depends on the personality and character of the individual and the extent of depression. Often, a professional counselor or psychiatrist is needed to help decide which treatments are best.

SUICIDE

Just as burnout, rather than being a form of stress, is really the end result of unrelieved stress, suicide is the result of other factors and is not a mental or mood disorder in itself. It is important to look at suicidal behavior as a symptom of something deeper rather than a cause in itself.

Studies have shown that individuals who commit suicide are more likely to have experienced some traumatic life event. If you experience traumatic events in your life, it is important to get counseling, develop social support groups and become involved in other activities so that you do not isolate yourself during your ordeal.

Interviews with suicidal patients show that many had bouts with depression shortly before their suicide attempts and felt a sense of hoplessness and futility in dealing with life situations. :60 second managements for depression also can be utilized in dealing with suicidal possibilities.

Healthy individuals who feel good are less likely to contemplate suicide than those who have a chronic illness. This is especially true for older patients with chronic pain or individuals who believe their illnesses are serious. If you have physical problems and are beginning to become depressed over them, you need to seek professional counseling, as well as to get differing opinions from other physicians.

Aside from professional advice, learning to cope with stress and depression by using all the channels available is the best way to bring about a healthy attitude and prevent suicidal stress reactions.

SCHIZOPHRENIA

Schizophrenia is actually a group of mental disorders related to the thinking process. It includes symptoms such as delusions, hallucinations, and extreme withdrawal from society and other people. Like depression, schizophrenia may have a number of different causes including environmental factors and genetic predisposition. In many cases, however, people on the verge of schizophrenia have been shown to experience severely stressful events which precipitate and trigger the disorder.

In the past, stress wasn't even considered a factor in the development of schizophrenia. It is now believed that individuals who are vulnerable to schizophrenia may succumb to it because stress actually precipitates it. And even though many cases of schizophrenia are caused by something other than stress, we can't ignore the fact that stressful life events are commonly found prior to the onset of the disease itself. Standard therapy usually involves the participation of family members, relatives, and social support groups.

The emotional stress associated with being the parent, spouse, or relative of a schizophrenic can be even greater than the stress experienced by the schizophrenic. Because of this, the benefits of support groups for family members are enormous. In these groups, stress is relieved by putting problems into words and talking about them. Often, high tension events are defused because individuals are once again able to cope with situations that they couldn't deal with alone. Social support is an important part of schizophrenia treatment because it involves relationships and activities which act as buffers against stressful life events.

SEXUAL DYSFUNCTION

One of the leading causes of sexual problems is emotional stress. In many cases, simply recognizing the source of stress is enough to bring about complete recovery. On the other hand, failure to recognize stress as a cause can lead to serious emotional disorders and permanent loss of sexual desire.

In the male, both sex hormone and sperm production can be severely inhibited as a result of stressful experiences. Therefore, not only is the sex drive lowered, but fertility is significantly decreased. Sexual problems are especially stressful because they tend to spiral into a vicious cycle that grows worse and worse over time. Couples begin to find ways to avoid intimacy in order to avoid stress.

Two important stress managements that can lead to a solution are:

1. *Communicate.* Anyone experiencing sexual problems can become lonely and hostile. Couples need to know that they need to become partners in the treatment of stress. A man or

woman alone can seldom overcome the cycle of sexual deficiency without cooperation from his or her partner. In many cases, the relief of sharing the stress, fear, and anxiety is enough for complete recovery.

2. *Use special exercises to help reverse sexual problems.* There are several excellent books which discuss sexual problems, their causes and their cures. Don't be afraid to experiment.

Sexual problems in themselves are a tremendous source of stress. Becoming impotent or frigid can easily lead to depression and anxiety and cause illnesses such as ulcers, which may develop into more serious problems. It's impossible to say how many good marriages have broken up because couples didn't realize just how much stress can affect their sex lives. If there's one action we can take, it's to include our spouse or be included by our spouse in order to gain the strength needed to overcome a problem that usually can't be dealt with alone.

Whenever we encounter a stress-related sexual problem, we need to remember three things: (1) with high expectation comes occasional failure; (2) with occasional failure should come understanding, compassion, and a sense of unity; and (3) with understanding and unity comes communication and a deeper awareness of one another's needs. It's only through understanding, compassion, and communication that we truly begin to rid ourselves of the sexual problems that are driven by negative stress responses. If we can do that, we'll experience the joy and satisfaction of finally knowing that sexual freedom lies not within the bounds of bedroom walls but within ourselves!

MENTAL HEALTH IN
VIETNAM VETERANS

The mental health problems of Vietnam veterans are unique in a number of ways. They've had to deal with the emotional trauma of participating not only in an unpopular war but in a war that made them the brunt of hostility and criticism. As a result, many men still suffer from severe emotional damage from the war as well as from the psychological abuse they received when they finally returned home. Today, we look at Vietnam veterans differently than we have in the past; but thousands of veterans are still carrying the emotional scars of rejection. They need the benefits of social support groups in order to cope with the stress in their lives.

This pattern of psychological stress in veterans also has been seen in previous wars. When we look at past mental health records, we find that during World War II as many as 500,000 individuals were discharged from the military because of psychological reasons. It's not even known how many of those veterans continued to have emotional problems—or how many continue to have emotional problems even today.

When comparing the various types of coping strategies, it was found that positive social support had the biggest influence in helping veterans deal with post wartime stress. In some cases, intense psychiatric help is needed in order to alleviate severe stress disorders. In general, however, some of the most effective coping strategies are:

1. Developing and mastering interpersonal relationships. This can be done by using behavior and attitude modification to improve one's outlook; learning communication skills to interact with others; and participating in outside activities to develop a social support network.

2. Joining veterans groups and organizations. Groups that include people with similar experiences are a good way to cope with stress because you can "talk things out" with others who really know what you're going through.

3. Using positive reinforcement strategies to improve self-image, raise low self-esteem, and condition the brain to respond in a positive and constructive way.

SEASONAL AFFECTIVE
DISORDER (SAD)

One of the most recent discoveries has been the phenomenon in which individuals become depressed, sometimes severely, as a result of not being exposed to enough light. Individuals with SAD are normally affected during the winter months when photoperiod is shortest and in temporal geographic areas where the dark phase of the dark–light cycle is prolonged (Australia, for example). The pineal gland, located in the brain, releases a hormone called melatonin, which we now know can alter moods and behavior. Melatonin is inhibited by light. Whenever levels of melatonin begin to decrease as a result of decreasing light, some individuals begin to suffer a series of symptoms that often are mistaken for depression. Symptoms of SAD vary from individual to individual, but according to experts, the most common symptoms include:

Sadness	Withdrawal from others
Depression	Increased periods of sleep
Irritability	Decreased sexual activity or desire
Anxiety	Increased appetite
Fatigue	Weight gain
Sluggishness	Craving for sweets
Restlessness	Moodiness

These symptoms may be continual throughout the Fall and Winter and disappear completely during the Spring and Summer months. Many SAD patients don't actually regain their full energy and activity levels until the summer months when the photoperiod is longest. Increasing the short winter photoperiod by adding artificial bright light can reverse symptoms of SAD within a few days.

If you're affected by SAD, you may be able to reverse your symptoms by exposing yourself daily to special fluorescent light, which must be much brighter than normal indoor illumination. The SunBox company manufactures special high intensity fluorescent lighting, which has been effective in curing over 80 percent of all SAD patients. Your physician is in the best position to diagnose SAD and can prescribe a daily treatment regimen that's right for you. He or she can also tell you how you can obtain the special light you need.

PREMENSTRUAL
SYNDROME (PMS)

PMS remains a controversial subject because no real concrete evidence has been found to indicate its causes. Many experts, however, feel that PMS is linked to periodic hormonal changes and, thus, place it along with SAD and some forms of depression in the category of biorhythmic disorders. PMS also may be caused or triggered by changes in brain chemicals prior to menstruation or as a result of social or environmental factors such as severe stress events. Symptoms of PMS include:

Water retention	Lethargy and fatigue
Depression	Crying spells
Anger	Increased appetite
Irritability	Weight gain
Anxiety	Craving for sweets
Negativism	Emotional upheavels
Acne	Headaches

Most women notice at least some of these symptoms shortly before menstruation. PMS, however, refers to the more severe symptoms in which women can virtually become disabled as a result of intense emotional, behavioral, or physiological changes. The most recent studies have shown that PMS can be treated with hormone therapy or with diuretics. In many cases, however, symptoms of PMS have been dramatically relieved with a combination of exercise, diet, and changes in certain habits. The following are 4 important strategies that can be used to relieve PMS symptoms for many women.

1. Exercise regularly.

2. Maintain a well-balanced diet.

3. Cut down on caffeine.

4. Eliminate cigarettes and alcohol.

LONELINESS

In today's society, loneliness is often the result of detachment, broken homes, and divorce and does not necessarily result from being alone or isolated.

According to experts, the key to overcoming loneliness is to reach out and give yourself the opportunity to grow with others as well as grow within yourself. There are several effective stress repressors leading to :60 second stress managements:

1. *Develop a wide variety of interests.* The worst thing you can do is sit and dwell on how lonely you feel and how few friends you have. Get out. No one has ever increased their circle of friends by avoiding contact with people.

2. *Become a volunteer.* By reaching out and serving others, you'll get your mind off your loneliness; keep busy, feel great about yourself and you will come to realize there are others less fortunate than yourself.

3. *Develop your introverted side.* It is important for you to learn to enjoy your own company, so that you don't feel an urgent need to be around others in order to keep from being lonely.

MUTUAL HELP GROUPS

For many of our problems, there are no easy answers or simple cures, but there are alternatives to coping alone. Mutual help groups can aid us in finding the hope and personal support we need because they offer us the most important outlet for recovery—the understanding and help of others who've gone through similar experiences.

Mutual help has been practiced since families first existed. As social beings, all of us need to be accepted, cared for, and emotionally supported. We also find it very satisfying to care for and support those around us. Within the most natural mutual help networks—our families and friends—we establish the one-to-one contact so important to our happiness and well-being. This informal support is such a basic part of our social character that we're apt to take it for granted, but it clearly influences our ability to handle distressing events in our lives. Many of our daily conversations are actually mutual counseling sessions whereby we exchange the reassurances and advice that help us deal with routine stresses. In fact, research scientists have found that there's a strong link between the strength of our social support systems and our health.

The personal support we receive from family and friends, however, is only one part of the support network that helps sustain us through life. As we develop socially and intellectually, we tend to associate with others who have similar interests and beliefs. In groups such as religious congregations, civic and fraternal organizations, and social clubs, members benefit from a shared identity and a sence of common purpose. Through combined efforts, these groups often can promote or accomplish what the individual, acting alone, cannot. Our reasons for joining groups may vary considerably, but each member's presence and participation adds to the strength of the group. Thus, the group becomes an instrument for service to the total membership.

There are a number of ways to get information about mutual help groups. Some of the larger ones are listed by subject in the phone directory, and the names and phone numbers of many more are available from hospitals and local mental health and social-service agencies. Directories of mutual help groups usually can be found in public libraries. As an introduction, I've listed some of the more common mutual help groups in the back of the book.

Throughout this chapter, one coping strategy stands out more than any other, and that is the idea of developing social support systems and becoming involved with other people. No other stress therapy has had so much impact on so many different emotional problems. As a society-oriented people, we need other people to relate to and to communicate with. Without this part of our existence, most of us would be unable to deal with the mounting stresses that we're constantly subjected to at work and at home.

We can't be individual islands and expect to survive emotionally in a society that places such a premium on social support. When we deny ourselves the opportunity to interrelate with others, we're diminished because we don't allow ourselves to be involved with humankind. We're all part of the main—society in general and our community in particular. Unless we take advantage of our strong human need to have relationships with other people and become involved with one another, we'll continue to have high rates of stress-induced adult and childhood disease, mental health problems, and suicide. In our stress-filled society, we all have a stake in each other's lives.

· Chapter 7 ·

Childhood and
Adolescent Stress

Adults don't have a monopoly on stress. In fact, childhood can be a time of tremendous anxiety and emotional upheaval. The reason children seem less stressed than adults is that they're normally more resilient and less likely to succumb to illnesses and diseases caused by stress reactions. Rather than exhibiting physical symptoms (even though physical symptoms do occur), children usually respond to stress with overt emotional and behavioral problems. These problems may be a strong indicator that your child is experiencing some sort of stress in his or her life. The following is a list of the most common life change events typically experienced by children and which can be serious sources of stress:

STRESSFUL LIFE EVENTS
FOR CHILDREN

I. EVENTS EXPERIENCED BY PARENTS

Death of a parent

Separation of parents

A parent who is an alcoholic or abuses drugs

Parent out of work who is usually employed

Marital reconciliation for separated parents

A divorced parent begins to date or remarries

Parent in jail or prison

A parent remains depressed for an extended time period

II. EVENTS EXPERIENCED BY THE FAMILY

Death of a sibling or extended family member

Prolonged separation from parent

Severe illness of a family member

Birth of a sibling

The addition of a new person to the household

A sibling leaves home

Death of a pet

Change in residence

Lack of supervision for prolonged periods

Family financial problems

Vacation with the family

III. EVENTS EXPERIENCED BY THE CHILD

Serious physical illness or injury or hospitalization

Sexual abuse or exploitation by an older, bigger person

Physical abuse including harsh physical punishment

Emotional abuse

Physical abnormality or deformity

Beginning or ending school

Being retained or accelerated a grade in school

A change in recreation—starting a new sport in school

Outstanding personal achievement

Change in eating habits

Being picked last by a team or group

Going to the dentist or doctor

Starting physical changes or puberty

Starting to date

Toilet training

Difficulty making and keeping friends

Many life changes experienced by children involve problems within the family such as divorce, illness, or death. Therefore, a child who doesn't necessarily experience personal stress directly still will be stressed as a result of the parent's stress. As parents, we need to be aware of how even small life changes or personal problems can affect our children, who are keenly in tune with everything that's going on in their home environments.

Just as adults experience stress symptoms, children under stress will exhibit certain symptoms that manifest themselves as behavior or personality problems. You should watch for key symptoms such as excessive crying, withdrawal, aggression, or regression. Other key symptoms to be particularly aware of are:

I. PHYSICAL SYMPTOMS

Sleep problems such as insomnia, sleep walking, or excessive sleep

Eating or weight problems

Excessive crying with no provocation

Teeth grinding—asleep or awake

Clumsiness or accident proneness

Listlessness or fatigue

Nervous tics such as muscle twitching, nail biting, eye blinking, etc.

Bed wetting (especially older children)

Nightmares

Stuttering or stammering

Difficulty concentrating or easily distracted

II. BEHAVIORAL SYMPTOMS

Regression to younger behaviors

Failure in school

Cruelty to animals or people

Stealing

Running away

Destroying things

Lying or cheating

Temper tantrums

Excessive daydreaming

Perfectionistic—must have everything exactly right

Drug abuse

III. RELATIONAL AND SELF-ESTEEM SYMPTOMS

Withdrawal or unwillingness to try

Feelings of hopelessness

Referring to oneself as dumb, stupid, or incapable

Making suicidal statements like "I want to die" or "I wish I was never born"

Excessive fears

Loss of friends

Other children avoid or act as if he/she were wierd

Does not join in group activities

:60 SECOND STRESS MANAGEMENTS FOR CHILDREN

All normal children have some of these symptoms at one time or another, but if your child exhibits several of these symptoms simultaneously or for prolonged periods of time, you may need to take a closer look at what it is that's causing these symptoms. Sometimes a professional is needed to identify and assess the reasons or causes for stress and to prescribe specific stress management techniques designed for children. But as a parent, you may want to try the following nine strategies in order to help your children better manage their stress:

1. *Moderate your child's activities.* Never allow children to take on too many activities at the same time. Whether they're involved in sports, academics, or work, children need to pace themselves just like adults in order to prevent

burnout and keep from developing stress symptoms. But unlike adults, children aren't as able to manage their time efficiently and can't cope with activity overload. Moderating their activities will help your children maintain a more balanced and stress-free lifestyle.

2. *Show your children physical affection.* One of our more basic human attributes is our need to be touched, hugged, and kissed. Children especially need to be held during times of stress so that they feel reassured and safe. Telling your children how you feel and how much you love them also will soothe their stress and at the same time teach them to verbally communicate their feelings with others.

3. *Teach your children proper assertiveness.* Your children need to know how to deal properly with angry feelings, how to cope with criticism, how to say no, and how to stand up for themselves. Assertiveness is simply a way for children to express their feelings openly so that lines of communication are open and stress doesn't build up. By expressing themselves verbally, children also will feel more in control and thus reduce their need to act out negative behavior.

4. *Give your children the attention they deserve.* All children naturally thrive on attention. So make certain that your children are praised regularly and listened to. Whenever children sense they're being ignored, they begin to exhibit undesirable behaviors in order to get attention. Paying attention to your children is one of the best ways to assure them that you really care about what they're doing and how they're feeling.

5. *Set reasonable goals.* In order to prevent the stress of failure, don't expect perfection from your children. Whenever you expect too much from anyone, you automatically set them up for potential failure and make them feel that what they do is never good enough. So, instead of criticising small failures, tell your children how much you appreciate their efforts and accomplishments. This praise will perpetuate

success because your children will naturally want to be praised again and again.

6. *Be a role model.* Actions truly speak louder than words. If you deal with anger appropriately, chances are your children will also. If you show affection, share and cooperate with others, and communicate feelings properly, your children will as well. Research has even shown, for example, that the values you set for your own health such as drinking, smoking, diet and exercise will leave a lasting impression on your children and instill in them similar values. Therefore, never underestimate the power you have as a positive role model and the influence you wield in molding your children's behavior.

7. *Ease tension through humor.* Humor is a great stress reliever and is one of the best ways to break tension and anxiety. Maintaining a good sense of humor also will teach your children to develop their own sense of humors and, consequently, will give them a tool they can use to manage their own stress as adults.

8. *Encourage independent thinking.* As adults, one of the reasons we become stressed is our inability to work out solutions to problems. More than likely this inability is the result of our not being allowed to do things in our own way and to solve problems independently as children. So instead of trying to work out everything for your children, encourage them to spend time thinking about their problems independently and working through them until they reach solutions. This doesn't mean you shouldn't be there for assistance and support, just that you should really make an effort to help your children think for themselves and learn to come up with intelligent answers.

9. *Spend quiet time with your children.* Spending quiet time with your children will not only help them wind down after a busy day, it also will teach them how to relax. As parents, it's important to be an example to your children so that they grow up having a good sense of how to cope with the stress and anxiety in their lives.

:60 SECOND STRESS MANAGEMENTS FOR HELPING CHILDREN COPE WITH SCHOOL

The first day of school is a milestone in your child's life. It also can be a very traumatic and stressful time of life because environment. Your understanding at this "turning point" is important to the child's future attitude toward school and to his or her healthy growth and development. Experts in child mental health and development emphasize that you, the parent, can play an important role in starting your child off with the self-confidence needed throughout life. This self-confidence is built upon good feelings about parents, about authority figures at school, about other children, and about himself or herself as a worthwhile human being.

To help your child cope with school, especially during the early stages when he or she is just beginning, here are some suggestions that can ease the transition from the home environment and make school less stressful from the start.

1. *Make the first day of school an important event.* Starting school is the first major separation from the secure and familiar world of home and family. It marks entrance into a new universe of friendship, learning, and adventure. You as parents can never again share completely in this world and, therefore, your greatest gift to your child at this time is your loving support and understanding. Make this day special and exciting.

2. *Prepare your child for the new experience.* Explain to your child what to expect by answering all questions honestly. Children need to know the number of days and the length of time they'll be in school, as well as how to get there and back. A child may be anxious and needs to know details in order to handle the stress involved. Working mothers and fathers should make certain that the child knows the arrangements for before and after school care.

3. *Convey a positive attitude about school.* If you as parent show enthusiasm for what the school experience can mean, your child is more likely to look forward to it.

4. *Make transportation plans clear to your child.* If he or she is to walk to school, walk the route together a few times before and after school starts. If there are other children from your neighborhood who are the same age, see if they can walk together. If your child is going to school by bus, help him or her identify the vehicle. Encourage older children to watch over the younger ones. And once the bus arrives, be direct; say goodbye and allow your child to board alone. If your child cries, try not to overreact; in most cases the tears quickly disappear.

5. *Create a normal routine atmosphere at home the first few days of school.* Don't deny or avoid the uniqueness of the situation, but do take an active interest in what your child tells you about school when he or she comes home. Be a good listener, allowing time to talk about school and the people there.

6. *Give your child free playtime at home.* Now that your child spends more time in a structured school environment, you need to allow more free time at home for play. Otherwise your child will begin to associate school with a loss of playtime.

7. *Praise your child for the good things he/she has done.* Remember, there's more to be gained from accenting the positive. A pat on the back for the right answers can go a long way. Too often we tend to focus on poor performance and behavior.

8. *Treat going to school as part of the normal course of events.* Going to school should be treated as something that's expected of your child and accepted by you. If your child appears nervous about going to school, discuss his or her concern. Show understanding and offer encouragement. A calm, matter-of-fact, positive attitude is your goal. Don't argue the issue of school attendance; it's required by law.

9. *Plan your day so that you can spend time with your child.* Be available when your child needs you. Be sure there's time to talk about school and the happenings of each day.

10. *Avoid comparing your child's experiences with your other children's experiences.* Such comparisons can be harmful to a child's self-image. Each of us is different, and we meet life's turning points and experiences in our own way.

In rare instances, when a child does not accept school after several days, or when fearfulness and feelings of distress appear and persist, the child may have a problem. At this point, you should seek advice from the school guidance counselor, the teacher, your family physician, school psychologist, community mental health center staff, or others who may offer expert advice. But with firm, patient, reassuring handling of your child by you and your child's teacher, your child should soon feel very comfortable away from home and will make new friends quickly. The most important goals for your child during those critical first days of school are to develop feelings of self-confidence and security and to realize that this new part of his or her life is going to be a wonderful and adventurous experience.

:60 SECOND STRESS MANAGEMENTS FOR HELPING CHILDREN COPE WITH GRIEF

Of all the traumatic life experiences a child may face, the death of a parent may be the most traumatic of all. According to Alan Breier of the National Institute of Mental Health, adults who had lost a parent during childhood had a much greater incidence of depression, anxiety, and alcoholism than did adults who grew up with healthy parents. These adults were so adversely affected by their loss that the trauma remained with them their entire life. It's important to realize that children before the ages of seven or eight have little or no concept of what death is and, therefore, the sudden loss of someone very close to them can be a profound shock. Some children may be just as deeply affected by the loss of a grandparent, brother or sister, or other relative.

When a child experiences the death of a loved one, reactions can vary. Some children become aggressive, angry, and hostile while others become withdrawn and isolated. Other common symptoms to watch for include poor school performance, regressive behavior like bed wetting or thumb sucking, and depression. All these behaviors are a way for children to express just how much the death has had an effect on their lives. In order to help a child overcome his or her grief, here are a few strategies you can use to help ease the pain and sadness.

1. *Avoid other life changes.* Death is a traumatic enough life experience for a child. Don't add any more. At this point the most important thing to do for at least a few months is to make your child feel safe, secure, and stable. And that means no unnecessary moving, no family disruptions, no changing schools, no sudden lifestyle shifts, and no other major life changes that could make your child feel insecure and unstable.

2. *Express your feelings freely.* Regardless of how much you want to protect your child from pain, he or she needs to feel included in the grieving process. This inclusion makes your child feel like a real part of the family and gives him or her a sense of belonging in every sense of the word. Naturally you don't want to be so emotional that you frighten your child into panic, but at the same time you don't want to exclude your child from what should be an intimately shared experience.

3. *Don't be afraid to talk about death.* Children are inquisitive by nature. They want to ask questions and they need to have answers. In many ways their fantasies about death and dying could be much worse than the reality of death itself. Let your children ask about death and communicate with them in a way that they can understand. Often, questions are a means of reassurance for children. By openly discussing death and answering questions, you'll be lessening their grief and giving them an avenue to vent their feelings and emotions.

:60 SECOND STRESS MANAGEMENTS FOR PRE-TEENS

Your child is in that "in between" age—old enough to understand many adult subjects, yet still young enough to willingly accept guidance from parents. This is a time when you can openly discuss the various stresses of life: peer pressure, alcohol, and drug abuse, as well as the relationships your child will have with others. You should take this opportunity to build a special rapport with your child so that communication is there when it is needed.

Stress managements are double-faced during these years. They will enable your child to cope with the pressures he or she will have to face in a very short period of time and they will ease the inherent worries a parent has over his child's ability to cope.

Several :60 second managements are:

1. *Rephrasing a child's comments to show you understand.* This is sometimes called "reflective listening." Reflective listening serves three purposes: it assures your child you hear what he or she is saying, it allows your child to "rehear" and consider his or her own feelings, and it assures you that you correctly understand your child.

2. *Watch your child's face and body language.* Often a child will assure you that he or she doesn't feel sad or dejected, but a quivering chin or too bright eyes will tell you otherwise. When words and body language say two different things, always believe the body language.

3. *Give nonverbal support and encouragement.* This may include a smile, a hug, a wink, a pat on the shoulder, nodding your head, making eye contact, or reaching for your child's hand.

4. *Use the right tone of voice.* Remember that your voice tone communicates to your child as clearly as your words. Make sure your tone doesn't come across as sarcastic or all-knowing.

5. *Use encouraging phrases to show your interest and to keep the conversation going.* Phrases such as "Oh, really?" "Tell me about it." "It sounds as if you . . ." "Then what happened?" are great for communicating to your pre-teen how much you care. If there's a pause in your conversation, use phrases such as these to encourage your pre-teen to talk.

6. *Give lots of praise.* Look for achievement, even in small tasks, and praise your child often. You're more likely to get the behavior you want when you emphasize the positive, and your praise will help your child have positive feelings.

7. *Praise effort, not just accomplishment.* Let your child know he or she doesn't always have to win. Trying hard and giving one's best effort is a noble feat in itself.

8. *Help your child set realistic goals.* If the child, or the parent, expects too much, the resulting failure can be a crushing blow. If a pre-teen who is an average athlete announces he plans to become the school quarterback, it might be wise to gently suggest that just making the team would be a wonderful goal and a big honor.

9. *Don't compare your child's efforts with others.* There will always be other children who are better and worse at a sport than your child, more and less intelligent, more and less artistic, etc. Your pre-teen may not know that a good effort can make you just as proud as a blue ribbon.

10. *When correcting, criticize the action, not the child.* A thoughtless comment can be devastating to a child. A pre-teen still takes an adult's word as law, so parents should notice how they phrase corrections.

   Helpful Example: "Climbing that fence was dangerous. You could have been hurt, so don't do it again."

   Hurtful Example: "You shouldn't have climbed that fence. Don't you have any sense?"

11. *Take responsibility for your own negative feelings.* One constructive way to share your own negative feelings about a situation is to use "I Messages." "I Messages" don't make children feel they are under attack or that they're intrinsically bad.

   Helpful Example: "Keeping the house neat is important to me. I get upset when you leave your books and clothes in the hall."

Hurtful Example: "You act like a pig sometimes. When will you learn to put things where they belong?"

12. *Give your child real responsibility.* Children who have regular duties around the house know that they're doing something important to help out. They learn to see themselves as a useful and important part of a team. Completing their duties also instills a sense of accomplishment.

13. *Show your chldren you love them.* Hugs, kisses, and saying "I love you" help your children feel good about themselves. Children are never too young or too old to be told that they're loved and highly valued. In families where parents are divorced, it's helpful if the nonresident parent also expresses love and support for the children. When the parent-child relationship is strong and loving, single parent families, including those where parents are widowed or unmarried, can give their children the same basis for self-esteem as two-parent families.

SIGNS AND SYMPTOMS
OF SUICIDAL BEHAVIOR

Recently, it was discovered that as many as 50 percent of all childhood and adolescent suicides may be disguised to appear as accidents. Since 1960, suicides for young people between the ages of fifteen and twenty-four have gone up nearly 300 percent! Five thousand adolescents die each year from suicides, but the frightening reality is that another 50,000 to 100,000 will attempt suicide unsuccessfully. The only reason why suicide remains the number two cause of adolescent death is that it's impossible to prove fatal car accidents (the number one cause of adolescent death) are a means of committing suicide.

In many of these suicide cases, depression was found to be the main component that triggered the suicide in the first place. Depression in these young people is usually the result of negative life events, most notably a high prevalence of broken homes, divorce, or separation. When suicide prone college students were surveyed, the reasons found for intending suicide were: high levels of severe life stress, hopelessness, and high levels of depression. Poor problem solvers exhibiting these symptoms were especially at high risk.

As adults, we tend to view adolescence as a period of friction, change, and problems. For the teenager, it's a very stressful time of concern about weight problems, acne, menstruation, late or early development, sexual arousal, school pressure, boredom, parental hassles, peer pressures, and money problems. It's a time of confused feelings, particularly in relationships with parents. Teenagers fight for independence yet fear too much freedom; they resent overprotection but need and want parental attention. Because the adolescent years are such a trying period, we often fail to recognize certain signals that indicate suicidal feelings or thoughts. Many times, these signals are a cry for help. Here are some warning signs to look for.

- Isolation and withdrawal from people, especially close friends

- Sudden or gradual loss of interest in appearance

- Unusual change in grades, school work, tardiness, or attendance

- Loss of weight and/or appetite

- Insomnia or excessive sleep

- Self-criticism, low self-esteem, feelings of failure, or sense of worthlessness

- Preoccupation with death and/or dying

- Loss of interest in previous activities and involvements

- Sudden accident proneness

- Sudden change in personality, especially involving apathy and depression

- Sudden angry outbursts, irritability, and hostility

- Excessive use of alcohol or drugs

- Sudden acts of risky or dangerous behavior like speeding in a car or running across a busy street

- Feelings of hopelessness or helplessness

- Suddenly giving away valuable or prized possessions

- Actual threats or verbal cues about not wanting to live anymore

For parents and teachers, it's a challenge to keep a balanced perspective on the teenager's emotional roller coaster ride. As young people bounce back and forth between childhood and adulthood, alternating irresponsibility with responsibility, parents and teachers often don't know what to expect. For this reason, it's even more important to be on a constant lookout for adolescent stress factors and for emotional and behavioral symptoms that may indicate trouble ahead.

The problem of stress-induced child and teenage suicide is especially tragic because, in many cases, the warning signs of depression and suicide are very evident but often overlooked. It's extremely important for families to realize that lines of communication have to remain open between parent and child. If a young person knows that the home is a place where feelings can be expressed freely and ideas shared and exchanged without criticism, that person will be able to deal with stress and depression in a more positive way. As the results of a questionnaire given to adolescents showed, most chose "talking to a friend" as the single most important act they could do to lessen the threat of suicide. Communication is the key. If we can put stress into words, we can begin to interact with one another and develop a bond that will have a tremendous effect on our ability to cope.

When asked about specific problems with parents, teenagers most often cite "not being listened to" as a major source of frustration and anger. Really listening to and communicating with teenagers is difficult and sometimes can be near impossible. But even though adolescence is a trying period, parents and teenagers must keep tuned in to each other to overcome one of the most difficult times in life.

STRESS AND
ADOLESCENCE

One of the greatest times of stress for families is the onset of
the adolescent or teenage years. For many families, these are
years of turmoil and strife, a period of transition in which newly
developing teenagers are honing their social skills and striving
for independence and freedom. In today's complex society,
these years can be more turbulent than ever before. The frightening reality of AIDS, drugs, voilence, and broken homes adds a
real dimension to stress that makes being a teenager one of the
greatest challenges a young person will face. But as much as the
stresses of life affect teenagers, they're not alone in their turmoil. If you're the parent of teenagers, you're equally affected,
and you need to deal effectively with both your teenager's stress
as well as the stress you feel as a result of your teenager's stress.

The first step in bringing some harmony back into your life
is to recognize that there are certain ideals and expectations
you have for your teenager that by themselves will naturally
create stress for you. The reason for this is simply that any lack
of control over your newly independent children is going to
make you feel uncomfortable. You might feel a sense of helplessness as you watch individuals for whom you've done everything for thirteen years suddenly want to do things by themselves and often in ways that seem strange and controversial.
This lack of control sets the stage for confrontation, intolerance,
and tremendous distress.

:60 SECOND STRESS
MANAGEMENTS
FOR PARENTS

If you're a parent of a teenager, you already know the
feelings of helplessness and frustration. But you'll develop a
greater tolerance—and, at the same time, create a more stress-
free home environment—by following some simple stress management control do's and don'ts.

DO'S
1. *Do* try to set a good example.

2. *Do* give your undivided attention when your teenager wants to talk to you.

3. *Do* try to listen calmly. Don't start preaching.

4. *Do* develop a courteous tone of voice. Respect brings respect. Try not to overreact.

5. *Do* avoid making judgments. Take an interest in your children's activities.

6. *Do* keep the door open on any subject. Respect the adolescent's desire for individuality and independence.

7. *Do* permit expression of ideas and feelings.

8. *Do* encourage self-worth. Build your teenager's confidence; don't degrade it.

9. *Do* be aware of how you treat other children in the family. Try to be fair.

10. *Do* make an effort to say nice things.

11. *Do* hold family conferences.

DON'TS

1. *Don't* expect your teenager to accept every rule and regulation you set forth.

2. *Don't* feel upset or rejected if your teenager tells you he or she hates you.

3. *Don't* try to be a perfect parent because none exist.

4. *Don't* blame your teenager's attitudes and behaviors on your problems.

:60 SECOND STRESS
MANAGEMENTS
FOR ADOLESCENTS

What responsibilities do teenagers have in decreasing the stress of adolescence and in bridging the generation gap? The following list of stress managers was formulated with the asistance of young people and adults. Have your child read them, tell him or her they were written with the help of teenagers, and then talk about them.

1. The first barrier of communication I must cast aside is the attitude of ignoring anybody over thirty. If I expect people to tune in to me, then I must be willing to talk to them.

2. Our generation wants understanding from our elders. In turn, it's only fair that we try to understand them. They have needs and feelings and reasons for their decisions.

3. I will listen to my parents with an open mind and look at the situation from their point of view. That's the way I would expect them to treat me.

4. I will share more of my feelings with my parents. They may have experienced some of the same problems. I need to give them a chance to help me.

5. I want my parents to express trust and confidence in me, to grant me more freedom and responsibility as I mature. It's necessary, then, that I live up to their confidence. What I do reflects on them, and they are held accountable for my actions and behavior.

6. Exercising the right to criticize my family, school, friends, or society includes the responsibility to suggest how practical improvements can be made.

7. To promote better communication in my family, I will practice courtesy and consideration for others. I will let my parents know I care about them. They're affected by pressures and problems of everyday living just as I am.

8. When I have a problem that I feel I can't handle, I won't keep it to myself. I'll be responsible enough to talk it out with my parents, and in return, they'll treat me with the respect and dignity I deserve.

Parents who have overzealous expectations of their teen-aged children, and who feel a desire to maintain complete control, are doomed to failure.

Certainly it's appropriate to guide, to set limits, to have groundrules, and to expect your teenagers to respect others. But if you want your family life to be less stressful and more even-keeled, you need to realize that you can't use the same strategies with your teenagers as you did with your younger children. They think differently, they feel differently, they act differently, and they require that you adapt a new attitude toward them. By giving up the idea of maintaining total control, you'll not only feel less anxiety and pressure, you'll also be sending a signal to your teenager that he or she is being given room to grow. That in itself will create less stress for your teenager and as a result even less stress for you.

No parent is perfect. There are times after a busy day at work when even the best parent would rather yell "Shut up!" than say "What I hear you saying is that you don't like what I cooked for dinner . . ." Luckily, children are tougher than we think. But we always need to keep in mind that regardless of age, all children experience the stresses of life and are just as prone to stress reactions as we are. And since they are in our care for only a short period of time, we must ensure that they too are able to cope with their stress before it has a lasting negative effect on their health and well-being.

Chapter 8

Stress and Aging

No one has been able to determine how our bodies age or why we're genetically programed to live only a certain amount of time. We do know that, as aging continues, our bodies are less likely to respond to challenges and more likely to be affected by negative events and situations. Aging, besides being a physically stressful process, is a very emotionally stressful time of life.

Older people are likely to experience two kinds of stresses: those that are "normal" to aging and those that are imposed by the environment. The stresses of illness, such as personal loss, diminished income, retirement, and inadequate housing, interact with social stresses, such as prejudice and noncaring, to produce isolation, loneliness and depression.

One of the greatest psychological stresses for older individuals is knowing that there's no change in their ability to learn and carry out mental tasks. Yet, there is widespread bias against them in society and the workplace. This tremendous emotional distress causes depression, which is the most common mental disorder affecting aging individuals. As we age, we allow our negative perceptions of aging to shape our behavior and attitudes. Successful aging can be accomplished only if we eliminate those negative perceptions and learn to cope with the stresses of age in a positive way.

A :60 SECOND LIFE
SATISFACTION QUIZ

How successfully are you aging? Here are some statements about life in general about which older people feel different. Read each statement carefully and, if you agree with it, put a check mark in the space under "AGREE." If you don't agree with the statement, put a check mark in the space under "DISAGREE." If you're not sure one way or the other, leave the spaces blank. At the end of the list is a scoring key that will give you an idea of how successful you are at aging well.

	AGREE	DISAGREE
1. As I grow older, things seem better than I thought they would be.	_____	_____
2. I've gotten more of the breaks in life than most people I know.	_____	_____
3. This is the dreariest time of my life.	_____	_____
4. I'm just as happy as when I was younger.	_____	_____
5. My life could be happier than it is now.	_____	_____
6. These are the best years of my life.	_____	_____
7. Most of the things I do are boring or monotonous.	_____	_____
8. I expect some interesting and pleasant things to happen to me in the future.	_____	_____

9. The things I do are as interesting to me as they ever were.   ____   ____

10. I feel old and somewhat tired.   ____   ____

11. I feel my age, but it doesn't bother me.   ____   ____

12. As I look back on my life, I'm fairly well satisfied.   ____   ____

13. I wouldn't change my past life even if I could.   ____   ____

14. Compared to other people my age, I've made a lot of foolish decisions in my life.   ____   ____

15. Compared to other people my age, I make a good appearance.   ____   ____

16. I've made plans for things I'll be doing a month or a year from now.   ____   ____

17. When I think back over my life, I didn't get most of the important things I wanted.   ____   ____

18. Compared to other people, I get down in the dumps too often.   ____   ____

19. I've gotten pretty much what I expected out of life.   ____   ____

20. In spite of what people say, for most of us, things are getting worse, not better.   ____   ____

21. I think about my age so much that I can't sleep.   ____   ____

22. I get angry more often than I used to.   ____   ____

23. I have as much pep as I did last year.   ____   ____

24. I see enough of my friends and relatives.   ____   ____

25. Many times, I feel that life isn't worth living.   ____   ____

26. Life is hard much of the time.   ____   ____

27. I'm not afraid of very many things now that I'm older.   ____   ____

28. As I get older, I feel less useful.   ____   ____

29. Compared to other people my age, I keep pretty active.   ____   ____

30. I don't usually feel lonely.   ____   ____

Score one point for each response that indicates life satisfaction. The appropriate life satisfaction responses for each statement are:

1. Agree   3. Disagree
2. Agree   4. Agree

5.	Disagree	18.	Disagree
6.	Agree	19.	Agree
7.	Disagree	20.	Disagree
8.	Agree	21.	Disagree
9.	Agree	22.	Disagree
10.	Disagree	23.	Agree
11.	Agree	24.	Agree
12.	Agree	25.	Disagree
13.	Agree	26.	Disagree
14.	Disagree	27.	Agree
15.	Agree	28.	Disagree
16.	Agree	29.	Agree
17.	Disagree	30.	Agree

Scoring key: 25—30 *High Life Satisfaction:* You're aging very successfully because you don't let your age get in the way of enjoying life. You have positive attitudes and a good outlook that keep you young at heart.

15—24 *Average Life Satisfaction:* You need to work on your attitudes and participate in more activities. There are times in your life when you could become more committed. Make sure that negative attitudes and behaviors don't begin to affect your health and well-being. Try to improve on those areas that you scored low on.

0—14 *Low Life Satisfaction:* You're not aging successfully at all. You need to begin taking immediate steps to improve your overall mental attitude and start participating in activities. Your goal should be to join clubs, do volunteer work, or do anything else that will turn your life around. Becoming involved should be the first step in transforming your unsuccessful aging into successful aging.

COPING WITH
MID-LIFE CRISIS

As young adults, we use the phrase "mid-life crisis" as a kind of joke because we don't yet think about middle age as something in our immediate future. When we hit 30, we look at middle age as inevitable and begin thinking more seriously about how we're going to face that time of life. And by the time we turn 40, we finally realize that we're at the midpoint of our lives and what we thought of as an inevitable but distant event has finally arrived. For many of us, this event can be a very stressful, if not traumatic, period of life.

Men and women differ significantly in how they react initially to the onset of middle age. According to experts, a man often experiences anxiety, feelings of inadequacy, and depression over his failure to achieve the goals he set out to accomplish. He may become despondent over his career, which he feels is going nowhere or which he no longer enjoys. He may become even more despondent if he believes that he's too old to do anything else and that he'll spend the rest of his life doing exactly what he's doing. A woman, on the other hand, experiences more happiness and fulfillment. She may be less bored, less lonely, and feel much better about herself and her future.

Even though men and women may begin mid-life differently, they both end up discovering greater life satisfaction as they age. By the time they reach 50 or 55, men and women have usually gone through the worst periods of mid-life and really start to enjoy their lives once again.

The key to coping with mid-life crisis, and getting through that 40- to 50-year-old period, is to realize that middle age is not the end of a satisfying and productive life but that it can be the beginning of a wonderfully enjoyable and fruitful time when we can finally begin to do the things we've always been wanting to do. In today's society especially, middle age often is thought of as the time to experience new activities, explore unknown talents, and exploit new opportunities. The problem many of us face when we reach mid-life is not our physical or mental health, but in our inability or unwillingness to look at mid-life as 40 more years of accomplishing most anything we want.

There are four :60 second managements for approaching mid-life with a new set of attitudes.

1. *Pursue your interests.* Many older people learn to play musical instruments, take classes, begin painting, and pursue new hobbies because they no longer have to worry about establishing themselves in a career. Forget about being over-the-hill and think about what you plan to accomplish in the long years ahead.

2. *Become involved.* Getting involved with politics, social causes, charities, or hospital work will do wonders for your self-esteem, give new meaning to your life, and help you through those critical middle years.

3. *Plan for your future.* Instead of visualizing your future as bleak, visualize it as a time of continued opportunities and great possibilities.

4. *Take time out.* Mid-life is the time to breathe. You still have half a lifetime to accomplish your goals.

Many of us begin our adult lives not really exploring our other talents and ambitions. We go through life convincing ourselves that we must spend the rest of our lives doing only what we've been trained to do. As a result, we live with that gnawing question of whether or not we could have been more, accomplished more, or contributed more. You don't have to give up what you already have. But you do need to develop your "shadow" side if you ever expect to reach your full potential and feel fully satisfied that you've become all that you could be.

COPING WITH DEATH
AND DYING

From the minute we're born we begin to die. Even though as youngsters we grow and develop rapidly, we proceed nonetheless on a slow and irrevocable journey toward the end of our life. As we get older, death becomes more real and more certain. The death of friends, relatives, and acquaintances continually reminds us of our own mortality and makes us realize that we too must someday face the inevitable.

Encounters with death or dying are very stressful experiences not only for the person who is dying, but also for those of us who must cope with the grief of actually witnessing someone we love go through the dying process.

Each person is different. Those of us who don't cope well with other crises certainly will have trouble dealing with our own death, as well as the death of someone close to us.

If we're grieving for someone we love, a decrease in immunity can cause us to become much more susceptible to disease. It is not uncommon for individuals to become seriously ill following the death of a spouse. There are several techniques for establishing :60 second managements both for coping with your own grief and the grief of others.

:60 SECOND MANAGEMENTS FOR COPING WITH YOUR OWN GRIEF

1. *Express your emotions.* Crying, remembering, and talking are all part of a healthy grieving process and shouldn't be suppressed for the sake of "appearing strong." Normal grieving may take as long as a year or longer, but some individuals may go through short periods of grief for the rest of their lives. They describe their pain and loss as something that will be a part of their memory always, even though they resume otherwise very normal and meaningful lives. Psychotherapists have found that by expressing your feelings early and allowing your normal grieving process to happen quickly and naturally, you'll recover more rapidly and, more importantly, you'll resume a healthy and emotionally satisfying life.

2. *Seek out social support.* Grief often is intensified when we have to experience it alone. This doesn't mean you have to join every support group you can find. But you need to allow others to help you and give comfort to you even if it's just in the form of a brief visit. It's normal to want time alone with your grief, to recall memories, and to think about what has happened in your life. But the worst thing to do, especially during the early stages of grief, is to become isolated and withdrawn from those who are

willing to give you needed support. It has been found, for example, that women seem to cope better following a death because they tend to seek out support more often than men.

3. *Seek professional help.* Most of us who grieve will never need professional counseling. There is, however, a condition called "pathologic grief" in which bereavement becomes permanently stuck in the middle of the grieving process. We need to watch for symptoms like grief after a year of our loss, avoidance of anything associated with the death, severe anxiety, and depression. If your grief is not subsiding normally and is in fact causing you to exhibit more severe emotional symptoms, you need to get professional help in order to get through the grieving process and to keep you from developing even worse emotional problems.

:60 SECOND MANAGEMENTS FOR HELPING OTHERS TO COPE WITH GRIEF

1. *Be present.* Even though you may feel helpless in these situations, just your being there will be enough to give comfort. Someone who is grieving is more prone to depression, suicide, and emotional breakdowns and shouldn't be left alone for long periods of time. And even though grieving individuals want to spend time alone with their thoughts and emotions, they really do need support and love during the grieving process. An arm around a shoulder or a hug can mean all the difference in the world during an especially lonely moment.

2. *Be a good listener.* Part of a healthy grieving process is talking through the feelings of death and dying. Rather than discourage an individual's attempts to discuss death, listen and encourage an open and frank discussion of what has occurred. Talking actually can help speed up the grieving process and make recovery much less painful. When listening to a grieving person, never interrupt and say

things like, "it was really for the best," "there was nothing anybody could have done," or "now you can get on with your life." Try to be sensitive to the person's feelings, allowing him or her to verbalize grief without interrupting with statements that you think will lessen the impact of death.

3. *Be a source of activity.* Oten times, a grieving individual needs to get away and do things that will take his or her mind off the tragedy. Invite your friend for dinner, for a game of cards, to a movie, for a walk, to a concert, to a ballgame, etc. In some cases, it takes just a small push by someone who cares to get a grieving individual back on track and on the way to a speedy recovery.

4. *Be a continued source of support.* It's great to be a comfort to grieving friends when a death occurs. It's just as important to be there for them on a long-term basis. For many grieving individuals, the worst time following a death is the first anniversary or the first major holiday spent alone. To be a true source of support, you need to remember your friends on these critical occasions and invite them to dinner or to spend the day with you. If your friends want to talk about their grief, let them share their feelings and express themselves again. Your presence with them will reaffirm to them that they're not alone and can depend on friends for continued support.

:60 SECOND
MANAGEMENTS FOR
THE ELDERLY

Stress management for the elderly must include coping strategies that deal specifically with loneliness, physical disability, rejection, and feelings of worthlessness. Emotional stresses such as these are so powerful that older people often find it impossible to live or cope in a society that looks at them in any kind of negative way. Unless something is done, the stress of aging can become a destructive mental and physical process.

There's no question that social conditions affect physical

102

ability and independence and contribute enormously to the health of older people. Widowers and elderly, living in areas where there's no social organization for them, increase their chances of succumbing to illness and disease. On the other hand, older people belonging to religious groups or close ethnic groups are buffered against stress-related disease because they exist within a well integrated community. In essence, they have many social and community ties.

For some time, social isolation has been suspected of increasing the aging process. In one study, for example, it was found that people lacking social ties had three times the mortality rate over a ten-year period than people having close social ties. Being involved in social and community affairs, giving and seeking advice, and other forms of assistance had an important effect on how older people perceived their own health status. Furthermore, having close friends and confidants had a strong tendency to relieve stress and influence both physical and mental health. In another study, it was shown that the stresses of retirement, death of a spouse, and decreased activity were lessened as a result of having supportive exchange with an intimate friend.

Social support networks, then, serve to bring us back from isolation into a social community that will respond to our needs and offer us an outlet for sharing, communicating, and interacting. Some of the best social support networks are religious organizations, retirement associations and clubs, volunteer and charity organizations, and community action groups. These kinds of support groups can enrich our lives by making us feel useful and needed and by giving us a sense of dignity. Aging, after all, doesn't necessarily mean an end to our challenges but the beginning of a new phase of our lives in which we fulfill those challenges in a different but equally enthusiastic and satisfying way.

There are several coping strategies which will lead to :60 second managements that can help older people deal with the stress in their lives and slow down the aging process.

1. *Participate in "enrichment programs."* All these activities are a way to increase self-esteem and achieve something worthwhile.

2. *Participate in sporting activities and exercise.* Exercise helps

us boost our energy reserves and triggers the release of endorphins, which help us cope with both physical and mental stress.

3. *Obtain proper health care.* Minor health problems can lead to major health disorders. Never assume any kind of physical or mental illness is a normal byproduct of age.

4. *Get a pet.* Pets satisfy needs such as caring and a desire to be loved and needed. Animals fulfill the human craving for emotional relationships and promote interactions and involvement.

5. *Improve eating habits.* Eating right can have an anti-aging effect on the body. You'll experience fewer stress reactions and live a lot better.

6. *Eliminate destructive habits.* Smoking and alcohol consumption can be deadly for older people, since they can adversely affect the reaction of prescribed drug medications. Adverse drug reactions lead to negative stress reactions which can encourage even more smoking and drinking.

7. *Exercise the brain.* Some of the best writers, poets, painters, musicians, scientists and scholars are well past their '60s. We should never allow age to get in the way of our ambitions.

The evidence that stress can indeed accelerate the aging process is only now beginning to accumulate. As more and more long-term studies are done, it's becoming clear that stress reactions, especially stress hormone reactions, contribute to the deterioration of body tissues, breakdown of immune function, susceptibiilty to illness and disease, and acceleration of age-related structural changes in the brain. It's also clear that stress-induced activities and habits such as poor eating, smoking, drinking, improper drug use, etc. also have a tremendous influence on the overall aging process.

As we get older we need to be more aware of stress responses and be wary not to treat them as just "normal aging symptoms.". By using coping strategies, maintaining good health habits, eating properly, belonging to social support groups, and practicing relaxation exercises, we can actually slow down the aging process and live out our lives in the healthiest way possible.

· PART II ·

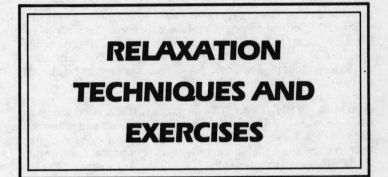

RELAXATION TECHNIQUES AND EXERCISES

Introduction

We have learned what happens to us during stress and how stress reactions bring about many kinds of illnesses and disease. We have discovered how our own habits shape behavior patterns and how we can establish :60 second management reactions.

There are various relaxation exercises that are the mainstay of any stress management strategy. No amount of attitude or behavior modification can totally replace relaxation as an effective tool for relieving stress. We know that what we do within the first few minutes of a stress reaction sets into motion the mechanisms of physical response. It is during these few seconds that we can change that response from a negative and destructive "stress response" to a positive and beneficial "relaxation response." The relaxation response is just as natural.

Our goal has been to develop and evoke the relaxation response so that it becomes a :60 second management instantly and automatically available.

The principal relaxation exercises are progressive muscle relaxation (PMR), tension relaxation, meditation and imaging. Once practiced and learned, relaxation exercises can bring our body back to a state of relaxation within 60 seconds, after which we can continue to relax for as long as we choose. Learning to eliminate negative stress reactions is the key element behind :60 second stress management.

Chapter 9

Progressive Muscle Relaxation

(PMR)

The principle behind relaxation training is that tension is incompatible with relaxation. In other words, we either do one or the other. Whenever we relax our mind and our body, we automatically exclude the tension that produces muscular tenseness. Therefore, relaxation exercises produce a feeling of well-being and rest by creating a relaxed state that actually inhibits anxiety and negative stress reactions.

The degree to which our muscles are relaxed can be controlled by practicing a special technique called "Progressive Muscle Relaxation" or PMR. In PMR, the objective is to induce deep muscular relaxation by gradually releasing tension from various parts of the body one part at a time.

There are three basic positions which facilitate any kind of relaxation exercise, including PMR. These are: (1) lying position (figure 9a); (2) prone position (figure 9b); and (3) semireclining position (figure 9c). The semireclining position is useful whenever we're at work or any other place where lying down isn't possible. Most beginners find that lying down is the most effective position because it's the one that evokes the relaxation response the fastest. After learning a relaxation technique, any position can be equally effective and satisfying.

Regardless of which position is used, comfort is absolutely critical. Pillows should be placed under the head, knees, and arms, as shown in figure 9a, or under the face, pelvis, and feet, as shown in figure 9b. In the semireclining position, the chair should be soft and comfortable and have cushioned arms. If necessary, the forearms should be supported by placing pillows

**Figure 9a
Lying**

**Figure 9b
Prone**

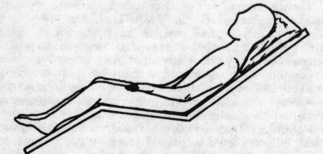

**Figure 9c
Semireclining**

on the chair arms. The feet also need to be supported either by a foot rest or a pillow. The head must be in a comfortable position and supported by a chair, cushion, or pillow. Unless the body is totally comfortable, relaxation will be possible but won't be as effective. Therefore, body position and comfort are the principle starting points to begin any relaxation exercise.

Some people have found that music is also a big factor in helping them relax because they can concentrate on the music and forget about other distractions. When listening to music, however, make sure that it's not too loud and never too harsh. Good music for relaxation is any type of soft, classical music by Handel (Largo, for example), Bach (Air on G String, for instance), Saint-Saens (The Swan, for example), or another favorite composition that's soothing, soft, and melodic.

After assuming a comfortable position, either sitting in a chair or lying down, take your shoes off, close your eyes and begin concentrating on your muscle groups one at a time starting with your toes first. Here's a sample of the kind of self-instruction you can use to produce a relaxed state. After using these instructions several times, you'll know them by heart and be able to use them automatically whenever you feel tense. You may even want to shorten the self-instructions after becoming adept at bringing on relaxation. As you begin to condition yourself to relax, you'll notice that relaxation will come more quickly and with much less effort each time. With enough practice, you'll be able to relax your entire body within a minute of starting an exercise.

PMR Self-Instructions

I'm falling into a nice, relaxed state; I'm breathing deeply, slowly, and smoothly . . . deeply, slowly, and smoothly. As I breathe, I'm becoming more and more relaxed . . . relaxed . . . relaxed. The toes on my feet are becoming numb; I feel a tingling sensation as the muscles in my toes become more relaxed and tension free . . . relaxed and tension free. They're getting more and more numb and heavy as I breathe. Each breath I take makes my toes become heavier and more numb . . . heavier and more numb. Now my toes are very heavy . . . very heavy . . . very heavy. The heavy, numb sensation is making my toes feel totally relaxed . . . relaxed . . . relaxed . . . more relaxed with each breath I take.

The numbness is beginning to creep up from my toes to my feet. My feet are beginning to tingle as they get heavy and numb . . . heavy and numb. There's a slight burning sensation in my feet as if they were submerged in warm, refreshing water. As I breathe, I can feel my feet becoming more numb and more relaxed. The muscles in both feet are becoming loose and soft . . . loose and soft; they feel very warm, heavy and relaxed . . . relaxed . . . relaxed . . . more relaxed with each breath I take. My feet are so warm and soft . . . warm and soft . . . relaxed . . . relaxed . . . relaxed . . . more relaxed with each breath I take.

I feel the warmth and numbness going to my calves as I breath and relax . . . breathe and relax. My calves are beginning to get very heavy and numb . . . heavy and numb. They're getting soft and warm as tension leaves and my muscles relax . . . relax . . . relax. With each breath I take, my calves are getting heavier and heavier . . . heavier and heavier, relaxed and numb, tension free and relaxed . . . relaxed . . . relaxed . . . more relaxed with each breath I take. The warmth is soothing and refreshing . . . soothing and refreshing, relaxed . . . relaxed . . . relaxed . . . more relaxed with each breath I take.

The numbness is going from my calves to my thighs. My thighs are now beginning to get warm and soft . . . warm and soft . . . loose and relaxed . . . loose and relaxed. My thighs are getting numb and heavy . . . numb and heavy; there's a tingling sensation as they become more numb and heavy . . . soft and relaxed . . . soft and relaxed. With each breath I take, my thighs are getting heavier . . . heavier . . . heavier. I feel the warmth and numbness creeping up my thighs and releasing tension. With each breath I take, my thighs feel more and more relaxed . . . relaxed . . . relaxed . . . more relaxed with each breath I take.

My fingers are beginning to tingle and get numb as the warmth creeps into them. They're becoming soft and loose . . . soft and loose, warm and numb . . . numb . . . numb. I sense a numbness going from the tips of my fingers into my knuckles as I breathe slowly and relax . . . relax . . . relax. The warmth and numbness is going into my wrists and my wrists are getting warmer and warmer, softer and softer. My hands are heavy and relaxed . . . heavy and relaxed. With each breath I take my hands are heavy and relaxed . . . relaxed . . . relaxed . . . more relaxed with each breath I take.

My arms are now beginning to get numb. The warmth is going from my hands into my arms and I feel heaviness and warmth . . . heaviness and warmth. As I breathe, my arms are getting heavier and heavier, numb and relaxed . . . numb and relaxed. A tingling and numbing sensation is going up my arms and releasing tension; my muscles are beginning to relax . . . relax . . . relax. My arms are very heavy now and relaxed . . . relaxed . . . relaxed . . . more relaxed with each breath I take.

The numbness in my arms is going into my shoulders. My shoulders are getting heavy and numb . . . heavy and numb. I can feel the warmth and heaviness loosening the muscles in my shoulders and they're getting more relaxed . . . relaxed . . . relaxed . . . more relaxed with each breath I take. As I breathe, tension is leaving my shoulders. They now feel very warm and numb . . . warm and numb, heavy and relaxed . . . relaxed . . . relaxed . . . more relaxed with each breath I take.

Warmth is spreading from my shoulders into my chest. My chest feels warmer and warmer . . . looser and looser. With each breath I take, my chest is becoming heavy and numb . . . heavy and numb, soft and relaxed . . . relaxed . . . relaxed. I can feel the muscles in my chest tingle and become numb and heavy . . . numb and heavy. As I breathe, tension is leaving and my chest is relaxed . . . relaxed . . . relaxed . . . more relaxed with each breath I take. My chest feels very heavy and numb now. With each breath I take, my chest is relaxed . . . relaxed . . . relaxed . . . relaxed.

The numbness and warmth are traveling from my chest to my neck. My neck is becoming warm and numb . . . warm and numb. I can feel the tingling, numbing feeling in my neck as I breathe and relax . . . relax . . . relax . . . relax. My neck is getting heavier and heavier . . . warmer and warmer . . . more relaxed with each breath I take. The tension is leaving the muscles in my neck and my neck is relaxed . . . relaxed . . . relaxed . . . more relaxed with each breath I take.

My face is getting softer and softer . . . softer and softer. The warmth is spreading from my neck into my face and it's getting warmer . . . warmer . . . warmer. As I breathe, my face is becoming heavier and heavier . . . relaxed and tension free. I feel all the tension leaving my facial muscles, and they're becoming relaxed . . . relaxed . . . relaxed . . . more relaxed with each breath I take.

My body feels warm and relaxed . . . relaxed . . . relaxed;

heavy and numb . . . heavy and numb. My body is so heavy and relaxed that it's sinking into the chair. Tension is melting away; my body muscles are soft and relaxed . . . soft and relaxed, heavy and limp . . . heavy and limp. As I breathe, I feel a soothing warmth and I'm relaxed . . . relaxed . . . relaxed. Tension is flowing away; With each breath I take, I can relax . . . relax . . . relax . . . relax . . . relax . . . relax.

This is only a sample of the kind of self-instruction you can use. You may use anything that comes to your mind, providing it elicits a pattern of gradual relaxation throughout your body. You also can continue and prolong the instructions so that you set your own pace and bring about relaxation in your own way. When using PMR, however, there are several things you should remember in order to enhance the technique. These are:

1. Always make comfort the starting point of relaxation. Remove your shoes and tight-fitting clothing, loosen your belt, and take off any jewelry that's going to distract you when you come to that particular body part. Don't try to practice relaxation in a room that's too cold or too hot. Remember, anything that can distract you probably will.

2. Speak to yourself in a slow, rhythmic, and monotonous manner. This helps get you into a steady pace, which facilitates relaxation.

3. Breathe slowly and rhythmically. It's important to use diaphragmatic breathing so that your breathing motion is smooth and uninterrupted. To make sure you're breathing properly, try this exercise. Place your right hand on your upper abdomen just above your navel and your left hand in the middle of your upper chest just above your nipples. When you breathe, the right hand should rise as you inhale and fall as you exhale; the left hand shouldn't move at all. After a few practice sessions, you should be able to breathe this way while having your hands at your sides in a relaxed state.

Don't exhale all your breath at the beginning of each breath cycle. Make sure that each breath is long and even, smooth and gentle. This rhythmic smoothness allows our autonomic nervous system to take over and keep us relaxed and tension free. When giving repeated self-instructions such as relax . . . relax . . . relax . . . say each word slowly at the same speed and smoothness as your exhaling breath.

4. Use "soft" words like relax, soothing, smooth, heavy, limp, numb, etc. Avoid words that are harsh and make you feel tense or lose concentration.

5. Don't go on to the next body part until the part you're working on is relaxed.

6. When your body is completely relaxed, allow yourself to remain that way for several minutes before getting up to stretch.

Progressive muscle relaxation has been very effective in relieving a variety of stress-related illnesses such as hypertension, migraine headaches, and ulcers. But even if we don't suffer from these kinds of illnesses, it may be necessary to use this technique several times a day if we're in severe stress situations. After a short while, relaxation will become much easier and almost spontaneous. We'll have conditioned ourselves to bring on the relaxation response just as we would any other natural, physiologic reaction. Once we learn how our muscles should feel when they're relaxed, it becomes a matter of habit and conditioning to bring them into that relaxed state whenever we want to. When we can do that, taking part in challenging and exciting activities will become much more enjoyable because we'll never have to fear the threat of muscle tension again.

Chapter 10

Tension-Relaxation

The principle behind tension-relaxation is to familiarize our bodies and minds with what tension should feel like compared with relaxation. This simple and easily learned procedure consists of conscious muscular tension followed immediately by relaxation.

The positions for the tension-relaxation technique are the same as those used for Progressive Muscle Relaxation. It's also important to be as comfortable as possible and not have any distractions or disturbances during the exercises. After practicing this technique daily for several weeks, the conditioning process will take over and our response will become easier and more automatic. Habits form that enable our muscles to relax at will regardless of the position we assume. The key element in shaping this conditioned response is our brain's innate ability to recognize degrees of physical tenseness and then to respond to that tenseness by relaxing the muscles almost involuntarily.

When first starting tension-relaxation exercises, different muscle groups are tensed individually during separate exercise sessions. These are: hands, arms, legs, chest, back, shoulders, neck, and forehead. Only after the individual muscle groups are mastered should you put the technique all together and use it to relax all the muscle groups in one session. By practicing the technique for each separate body region, the conditioning process is much more effective and total body relaxation will become much easier. Later, some of the muscle groups, such as hands and arms, shoulders and neck, can be combined so that relaxation is achieved by concentrating on only a few muscle groups.

Eventually, the tension part of tension-relaxation can be eliminated altogether because relaxation will become a classically conditioned response. You'll be able to relax your entire body at once or only the specific parts of your body that are especially tensed. A word of caution, however. Always be aware of your ability to recognize tension versus relaxation. That ability is the cornerstone of tension management and should always be your principle focus when trying to relieve tension in any part of your body. If you begin to have trouble doing that, go back to tension as a means of reconditioning yourself to again recognize the difference between the two muscle states.

The following are eight sets of tension-relaxation exercises, one for each muscle group. As you perform each exercise set, you should carry out the movement to its absolute limit before slacking off the muscle completely and resting. After reaching maximum contraction, stay tensed for at least ten seconds in order to get the full impact of what it feels like to become relaxed. Remember, the more tension you place on each muscle group, the greater the subsequent feeling of relaxation will be.

Practice Session #1—Hands

Tension: With hands at your sides, clench your fists as hard as possible. Keep them clenched for at least ten seconds. At first, you may want to tense only one hand at a time.

Relaxation: Release your hands and let your fingers slowly uncurl and go limp at your sides.

Note: Repeat this exercise three times, remembering to keep extending for at least ten seconds after maximum tension. After three sets, keep your hands and body relaxed and rested for twenty to thirty minutes.

Practice Session #2—Arms

Tension: Raise your arms and clench your fists very tightly for at least ten seconds. At first, you may want to tense only one arm at a time.

Relaxation: Allow your arms to fall limply to your sides. Your fingers should hang loosely and motionless.

Note: Repeat this exercise three times with maximum tension each time. After three sets, keep your arms very still and limp for twenty to thirty minutes.

Practice Session #3—Legs

Tension: Push your feet downward as far and as hard as you can for at least ten seconds. The toes of each foot should also be bent down at the same time.

Relaxation: Allow your feet and toes to go limp and to relax with your legs being very loose.

Note: Repeat this exercise three times with maximum tension each time. After three sets, keep your legs very still and limp for twenty to thirty minutes. Never cross your legs while doing this exercise.

Practice Session #4—Abdomen

Tension: Pull in your abdominal muscles as much as you can. Keep them pulled in for at least ten seconds.

Relaxation: Slowly release your abdominal muscles and lie perfectly still.

Note: Repeat this exercise three times with maximum pulling each time. Breath slowly and allow your abdomen to relax. After three sets, remain rested for twenty to thirty minutes.

Practice Session #5—Back

Tension: Arch your spine upward as far as you can until only your head and buttocks are touching the floor or bed. Keep your back arched maximally for at least ten seconds.

Relaxation: Gradually lower your back and let it become heavy and loose.

Note: Repeat this exercise three times. If necessary, place a small pillow underneath your lower back for more comfort. Remain relaxed for twenty to thirty minutes. This particular exercise is best done only in a fully reclined position.

Practice Session #6—Shoulders

Tension: Shrug your shoulders toward your head as hard as you can for a full ten seconds.

Relaxation: Release and lower your shoulders slowly. Let them rest limply and heavily.

Note: Repeat this exercise three times with maximum tension each time. After three sets, relax your shoulders and lie quietly for twenty to thirty minutes.

Practice Session #7—Neck

Tension: Push your head backward against a pillow or mattress as hard as you can for a full ten seconds.

Relaxation: Release your head and let it lie quiet and motionless.

Note: Repeat this exercise three times. Instead of pushing your head backward, you also can lift it forward as far as it will go for a full ten seconds before letting it drop back down to relax. After three sets, let your head remain relaxed for twenty to thirty minutes.

Practice Session #8—Forehead

Tension: Wrinkle your forehead as much as you can and hold it wrinkled for a full ten seconds.

Relaxation: Slowly release the forehead muscles and let your face relax completely.

Note: Repeat this exercise three times. It may be easier to tense the forehead muscles by frowning severely rather than wrinkling. You also can try to alternate wrinkling and frowning. After three sets, keep your face and head relaxed for twenty to thirty minutes.

When using tension-relaxation techniques, we need to follow certain rules and guidelines in order to make relaxation more effective and easier to learn. These are:

1. Try to set aside a specific time every day to practice, even if it's only a few minutes each day. The best times to practice are in the evening after a full day of tension or in the morning to help you get relaxed for the start of a day. However, be careful not to do exercises right before going to bed. If you wait until you're too tired, your mind won't be in the proper state to practice and the natural conditioning process won't be as effective.

2. Always wear loose, comfortable clothing when practicing relaxation techniques. Remove your shoes, loosen your buttons, and make sure you don't have anything around your neck. Also, remove jewelry such as watches and necklaces in order to prevent small distractions from ruining your practice session. Keep your eyes closed during the entire practice session and never cross your arms or your legs.

3. Try not to practice on a full stomach. During digestion, more circulating blood than normal is diverted to the gastrointestinal tract and away from muscles and other tissues. Lowered blood levels in muscles may cause cramps and discomfort during tension. Also, a full stomach will make you feel sluggish and keep you from concentrating as well as you should on the exercises.

4. Make sure you practice in a room that's quiet, well ventilated, not too well lit, and not too hot or cold. Any physical distraction will decrease the effectiveness of the exercises.

5. Muscles always should be relaxed slowly and gradually after tension, never abruptly. This will give you a better feeling of the transition between complete tension and complete relaxation. Let your body movements be smooth

and gentle, always flowing with your breath. During tension, never hold your breath—just let it flow naturally.

6. During each practice session, try to relax the muscle groups that you've previously worked on. For example, during practice session 3, while relaxing your legs, also relax your hands and arms. After the eighth practice session, you should be able to relax all the muscle groups each time you tense and relax individual muscle groups.

7. After muscles groups are tensed and relaxed, it may help you to actually visualize them becoming loose and limp—this is called "imaging." With smooth, rhythmic breathing, imagine your muscles becoming heavier and heavier. See them getting soft and tender. Give special attention to those muscle groups that are particularly difficult to relax completely. Most importantly, don't give up. Some days may be worse than others, and it's vital to repeat the tension-relaxation exercises daily at first so that relaxation becomes second nature.

Tension-relaxation is one of the best and most effective ways to learn relaxation because it conditions us to distinguish immediately between tensed and relaxed muscles. In other words, we actually acquire an ability to recognize even small degrees of tension within each individual muscle group.

Like PMR, tension-relaxation has been very useful in treating a variety of illnesses such as hypertension and migraine headaches. As a stress management tool, it's one of the best ways to train yourself to trigger the relaxation response whenever you feel tense or anxious. With practice, you'll be able to start relaxation at any stage of tension you happen to be in without ever having to contract your muscles at all. Depending on your physical and mental abilities, this may take anywhere from two weeks to two months. When you finally reach that stage, you'll have accomplished your goal of making relaxation a natural and spontaneous habit that becomes stronger and stronger every time you relax.

Chapter 11

Meditation

Meditation has been used for centuries in different parts of the world as a means of achieving deep relaxation and peace of mind. Although some meditative exercises use religious words and phrases, meditation itself is not a religion or a philosophy but a tool that utilizes our internal awareness to release tension.

There are four basic elements necessary for achieving deep relaxation through meditation:

1. *A quiet, peaceful environment.* Just like any other stress management exercise that produces relaxation, meditation requires solitude and comfort. Distractions must be avoided completely, perhaps more so than with any other technique because concentration is the most basic component of meditation.

    When choosing a place to meditate, make sure you find someplace that will be free from distractions for the entire length of your exercise. It may be a quiet room, a peaceful backyard, a church, or even the woods. The important thing is to make sure that you won't be distracted in the middle of your meditation.

2. *A decreased muscle tone.* Comfort is critical because any undue muscle tenseness will interfere with concentration. The best positions for meditation are the cross-legged sitting position on a firm pillow, mattress, or rug, or a normal sitting position on a straight, comfortable chair with your

head, neck, and back straight. Other positions, such as fully or semireclined, are not as effective with this particular technique because there's a tendency to become drowsy and fall asleep.

3. *A passive attitude.* This is probably the most important of the four elements because successful meditation requires that you not guide or direct your thoughts but let them go freely and passively. Nothing is more distracting during meditation than to think about everything that goes through your mind.

4. *A mental device.* In order to help concentration and keep distracting thoughts from interfering with meditation, you need to use a constant stimulus to focus on. A mental device is an object to dwell upon such as a sound, a word, a syllable, or a phrase that is repeated over and over during the course of the exercise. Because total concentration is one of the more difficult tasks we can encounter, using a mental device or a "mantra" allows us to break distracting thoughts and reach deeper levels of internal awareness.

:60 SECOND MEDITATIVE TECHNIQUES

The following are various meditative techniques that can be used to trigger the relaxation response. Try them all and then choose the one that best fits your personality and lifestyle. If you're not a religious person, you may not want to use a meditative technique that uses a religious word or phrase. On the other hand, if you are a religious person, meditation may be more effective and meaningful if it does involve a religious word or phrase. Whichever technique you choose, make sure it's the one that allows you to concentrate and become relaxed with the least amount of effort and the least number of distractions.

Meditative Exercise #1

Sit quiety in a comfortable position, close your eyes, and breathe through your nose. Become aware of your breathing pattern, and as you breathe out, say the word "relax" or "one" silently to yourself. Continue doing this for :60 seconds or so. When you finish, sit quietly for several minutes, at first with your eyes closed and gradually with your eyes open. Maintain a relaxed state throughout the exercise and allow relaxation to occur at its own pace.

Meditative Exercise #2

An example of a religious meditation is a repetitive prayer used by Christians as early as the fourteenth century. It's called "The Prayer of the Heart." Sit down alone, in a comfortable position, and in total silence. Lower your head, shut your eyes, and begin breathing gently and rhythmically while you imagine yourself looking into your own heart. Visualize your heart, and as you breathe out say "Lord Jesus, have mercy on me" or "God, grant me peace." Keep repeating this phrase over and over again each time you breathe out. If you like, you can change the phrase or use any phrase that suits your own personal attitudes and needs.

Meditative Exercise #3

This meditative exercise makes use of a rhythmic sound that you can focus on to time your breathing rate and to enhance concentration. Adjust a metronome to a slow setting, say 40 to 60 beats per minute and then begin an even breathing pattern that follows the beat of the metronome. Once your breathing pattern is established and you've begun concentrating on the click of the metronome, say the word "relax" at the same pace as both breathing and clicking. After doing this exercise for several weeks, your brain will automatically associate the metronome's beats with relaxation. Soon, you'll condition yourself to relax instantly because the metronome will act as a subconscious stimulus or cue that triggers the relaxation response.

Meditative Exercise #4

This meditative technique is also called autosuggestion because it uses some of the principles of self-induced hypnosis, although to a much lesser extent. Sit comfortably in a chair facing a wall about six to eight feet away. Pick a spot or an object on the wall (or place one there) that's about a foot above eye level. As you stare at the focal point, breathe slowly and rhythmically. Starting with the number ten, begin counting backwards, one number for each exhalation. As you count, continue to concentrate on the focal point and begin to feel your body getting more and more relaxed.

Soon after beginning the exercise, your eyelids will become heavier and start to blink. When that happens, just let them close. While your eyes are closed, continue counting, but now visualize the numbers in your mind as you say them silently. When you finally reach the number one, remain relaxed and let yourself feel free and easy. Remain in that position for ten to twenty minutes. When you're ready to come out, count from one to three. At one, prepare yourself; at two, take a deep breath; at three, open your eyes, stand up, and stretch.

Practicing this exercise will condition your brain to associate certain numbers (which act as cues) with certain stages of relaxation. Depending on your own individual pattern, number six may stimulate eye closing, number four may stimulate upper body relaxation, and number one may stimulate complete relaxation. The object of this meditation is to induce the relaxation response by suggesting to ourselves that certain numbers stimulate certain relaxation states.

Meditation can be a very effective tool in stress management because it teaches us not only to relax but to focus away from stressful thoughts and feelings. As long as we don't overdo it by meditating for hours on end, meditative exercises are safe and pleasurable; they bring balance to our body and peace to our mind. But most of all, they condition us to relax spontaneously by using devises such as sounds and objects as stimuli that trigger the relaxation response. Meditation has been around for centuries, bringing inner peace and tranquility to people of all religions and philosophies. We too can experience that peace and tranquility by using the power of our mind to eliminate the stresses in our body.

· Chapter 12 ·

Imaging Techniques
and Self-Healing

Imaging—also known as visualization or imaginal relaxation—makes use of mental images as a means of achieving a deeply relaxed state. After meditation, it's probably one of the oldest relaxation techniques practiced by mankind. In this type of exercise, vivid images associated with rest, tranquility, and serenity are used as positive feedback messages to the rest of the body. These images act as cues that stimulate the nervous system and cause tense muscles to respond subconsciously. Once practiced, imaging can be one of the simplest and most enjoyable of all relaxation techniques. And like other relaxation techniques, it too acts as a tool for triggering the relaxation response—in this case, by conditioning the brain to associate mental images with relaxation.

Imaging also has been used as a method for inducing self-healing. Because of its ability to shift the body's immune system into high gear, imaging has been used successfully to help treat various types of cancers as well as other diseases linked to a breakdown in the immune response. In combination with radiation or chemotherapy treatments, the use of imaging has resulted in much higher survival rates than with the use of treatments alone. This happens because "Natural Killer" cells, which are special cells that seek out and attack all types of cancer cells, are stimulated when the body is relaxed. Self-healing is possible when we allow the power of our brain to keep our immune system going at full force during those times when we need it most.

There are many different kinds of imaging exercises. The

type of imaging you do will depend on your personality and your experiences, as well as your likes and dislikes. But regardless of the imaging exercises you choose, you need to follow certain guidelines that will make them much more successful and enjoyable. These are:

1. Make comfort a priority before starting an exercise. It's almost impossible to maintain a positive image for any length of time unless you're relaxed and comfortable throughout the imaging session. Any tensions that arise will have a tendency to block or at least affect your concentration and, therefore, disrupt your image.

2. Make sure that the mental images you choose always "fit" your own idea of what's truly relaxing to you. If you hate the beach, for example, you shouldn't use an image of sand and sea as a relaxation device no matter how relaxing other people think it is. On the other hand, if you find a cool, lush green forest refreshing and relaxing, then use that as a mental image. Always use an activity, scene, or picture that makes you feel the most relaxed and gives you the greatest sense of pleasure and comfort. You're the only one who can do that.

3. Start each imaging exercise with relaxed and smooth breathing. Imaging is much easier once your mind and body are in the process of becoming relaxed. As you breathe and relax, concentrate on the evenness of your breath first and then begin visualizing. If you have trouble keeping an image in your mind, you need to reevaluate whether or not your chosen image is indeed the right one for you. There may be something in your image that's causing distractions or discomfort. If another image keeps cropping up in your mind, perhaps from your childhood or from a past vacation, then that particular image may be stronger and more effective than the one you've chosen. With practice, you'll be able to establish an image that's exactly right for you. Therefore, don't ignore images that keep popping into your mind if you find that they make you feel relaxed and peaceful.

4. Choose images that are vivid, real, and meaningful. Most of us have an idea of what we think the perfect image should be, but in most cases these fantasy images tend to become blurred and intermittent. The best images come from your own real experiences. Therefore, choose an image that you've experienced and enjoyed, one that has given you pleasure and peace. Because they're part of your stored memory, real images become more vivid and long-lasting and will serve you well time and time again.

:60 SECOND IMAGING EXERCISES USED FOR RELAXATION

There are literally thousands of examples of imaging exercises, each one as unique as the individual doing it. I'm going to give several examples here with the idea that you'll take the basic outline, change it if you like, and incorporate your own "personal image" into it. Although you may want to use one of the exercises given here, you should be aware of your own personal needs and desires in order for this stress management tool to work for you. Remember, it's very important for an image to "fit the individual" and not the other way around.

Imaging Exercise #1

Select a comfortable position, close your eyes, and begin breathing slowly and smoothly. With each breath, feel the muscles in your body becoming heavier and heavier. Imagine the tension melting away as you continue breathing rhythmically and naturally. Now picture yourself lying on a warm, tropical beach basking in the glow of an afternoon sun. Visualize the vivid, beautiful colors of the sky, the earth, the flowers, and the plants around you. As you lie on the beach, the warmth of the golden sand penetrates every pore of your body and makes you feel warmer and warmer. The golden sand feels soft and soothing; its warmth enters your hands and feet and begins to creep throughout your entire body. Imagine yourself lying serenely and restfully as your muscles become loose and limp. Feel your body sinking into the sand and drifting deeper and deeper into a state of peace and total relaxation. With each breath, watch your body become more and more relaxed, more and more at peace.

Now feel the warmth of the sunlight all over your body, warming you deeply and gently. Visualize the inside of your body bathed in the golden light, absorbing every ray and glowing as radiantly as the sun. A warm, gentle breeze swirls around your body and warms you even more. Visualize and feel the breeze blowing over every part of your body.

As you visualize these images, it may help to say to yourself: "I feel warm and relaxed, "I feel the warmth spreading throughout my body," or "the warmth of the sand is making my muscles feel so loose and relaxed." Continue the imaging exercise for about twenty minutes or so and then gradually become more alert, saying to yourself three times "I feel refreshed and relaxed." Slowly open your eyes, take a few deep breaths, and stretch for a few seconds.

Imaging Exercise #2

Select a comfortable position, close your eyes, and begin a smooth rhythmic breathing pattern. Continue breathing this way for a few minutes and then visualize a picturesque lagoon surrounded by tall palm trees and beautiful flowers. The water is a clear, blue turquoise and overhead is a blue cloudless sky. You hear nothing but the soft whisper of a breeze as it gently passes over your body and touches your face with its light invisible fingers.

Imagine yourself floating on the calm, gentle water. As you float, the warm water soothes and relaxes your muscles. Feel the water massaging first your feet, then your legs, your arms, and finally the rest of your body. The water becomes warmer and warmer, and as you drift deeper and deeper into a relaxed state, it begins to melt the tension away. Picture yourself absolutely weightless in the water, perfectly at peace and floating gently, smoothly, and slowly. You're one with the water; it surrounds you completely and loosens every muscle in your body. Each time you breathe, the warm, soothing water lifts you slightly; and each time you sink back down, more tension is melted away. Soon, your body is so relaxed in the water that you feel like you're a part of it.

You can do this exercise in a relaxed sitting or lying position or while taking a warm bath. A word of caution when

doing this in a bathtub, however. Since this technique will
make you feel so relaxed, you may have a tendency to doze off.
Make sure your head is propped up with a float or something
else that will prevent your head from slipping down into the
water. A sudden jolt like that can ruin your next attempt at
visualizing. Continue the exercise for about twenty minutes and
then visualize yourself slowly floating to shore. Gradually get
out of the water saying to yourself, "I feel so refreshed and
relaxed." Open your eyes, stand up slowly, and stretch for a few
seconds.

IMAGING AND
SELF-HEALING

For those of us suffering with illness and disease, the body
often is regarded as the enemy. Negative feelings and attitudes
are quite common during those trying times because we tend to
start thinking of our body as a source of distress rather than a
source of health and pleasure. We develop fears and anxieties,
which become worse and worse and lead to ever spiraling cy-
cles of depression and hopelessness. And we give up on ourselves because we just can't believe that the body that was
responsible for the disease in the first place is able to fight it at
the same time. Creating positive beliefs through imaging,
however, can reverse that cycle of fear and depression. Imaging
can actually stimulate our immune system to rise up and fight
disease head on!

The benefits of imaginal self-healing result from our positive expectations and attitudes toward illness. Together with
traditional medical treatment, which should always be a primary source of therapy, imaging can have a tremendous effect
on reversing the disease process while creating a mental environment that enhances the healing process. In summary, self-
healing exercises are effective because they:

1. Reduce the fear and depression of knowing that our body
   has been taken over by illness. By regaining a sense of
   control over our body's immune functions, we develop a
   more favorable outlook on our health, renew our energy
   levels, and establish a better perspective on life.

2. Bring about positive physical changes within our immune, endocrine, cardiovascular, and nervous systems. These changes act together to help fight illness and strengthen our ability to resist disease.

3. Condition our brain to respond to illness and disease in a natural and direct way. The process of relaxation by itself can decrease stress and tension to the point of completely altering bodily functions so they work for us instead of against us. By using the power of our mind to help fight disease, we enhance our ability to regain health and vitality.

The concept behind imaging is that total muscle relaxation and even self-healing are possible through the use of a simple mental tool—in this case an image. This mental tool gives us the power to trigger the relaxation response, maintain health, and stimulate the natural healing process within us. Again, we should never use imaging as the sole method of healing or disease therapy. Serious illnesses always should be treated by traditional methods, with relaxation and imaging used as important and beneficial aids in the overall treatment process. Each time you practice imaging, it will become easier to do and much more effective. Within a few weeks, you should be able to achieve deep relaxation and begin vivid imaging within a minute or so of starting an exercise.

The benefits of relaxation and imaging have been so great and the success rate so promising that more and more physicians are beginning to use this combined treatment as a means of enhancing therapy for a variety of illnesses and diseases. Practiced regularly in the comfort of your own home, imaginal relaxation is one of the simplest and most effective ways to relieve stress, maintain good health, and keep the immune system in a state of constant alert. As more and more is learned about how we respond to stress and about our body's natural defense system, we begin to discover that our body has an extraordinary power and ability not only to cope with day-to-day events but to literally heal itself in the process.

· PART III ·

SELF-HELP STRESS TESTS
AND EVALUATIONS

Chapter 13

Testing Your Stress Knowledge

How much more do you know about stress and how it affects you? The following stress tests are meant to reinforce your knowledge of stress and coping strategies and make you more aware of stress management as a tool for better living. If you answer a question incorrectly, go back to the section of the book that deals with that aspect of stress and read it once again. It's important to review those areas that you're unsure of in order to make stress management a complete and effective method for relieving the stress and anxiety in your life. If you answer all or most of the questions correctly, you can take heart in the fact that you're now your own stress expert and well on your way to becoming healthier and more stress-free.

FACTS ABOUT STRESS

	TRUE	FALSE
1. People react to emotional stress just as easily as they do to physical stress.	——	——
2. Constant arousal due to stress can cause a person's blood pressure to remain low.	——	——

3. Stress due to overload can
    result from demands that
    occur at home.   _____   _____

4. An individual who is ad-
    justing to many life
    changes in a short period
    of time is less likely than
    usual to become ill.   _____   _____

5. Thinking about an un-
    pleasant event is never as
    stressful as actually expe-
    riencing that event.   _____   _____

6. Thinking of oneself as use-
    less and powerless can in-
    crease one's stress level.   _____   _____

7. The most stressful situa-
    tions are usually those
    over which people feel
    they have a great deal of
    control.   _____   _____

8. Stress may decrease the
    body's ability to defend it-
    self against disease.   _____   _____

9. Severe stress may cause
    people to have accidents.   _____   _____

10. People who have Type A
    personalities are more
    likely to suffer from stress
    reactions.   _____   _____

11. One of the most common
    traits of Type A personal-
    ity is doing only one thing
    at a time.   _____   _____

12. Excessive stress affects the body's ability to utilize nutrients such as vitamins and minerals.   _____   _____

13. A person under stress may feel confused.   _____   _____

14. Overload occurs when people are able to meet the demands which are placed on them.   _____   _____

15. A person under stress is usually able to perform tasks better than usual.   _____   _____

16. Some degree of stress is necessary for life.   _____   _____

17. Stress disorders are caused by constant stress arousal, leading to organ system failure.   _____   _____

18. Too much stimulation is always more stressful than too little.   _____   _____

19. The stress produced by a situation depends more on the situation than on the person's perception of the situation.   _____   _____

20. The Type A personality is associated with heart disease.   _____   _____

21. The best level of stress is that amount which im-

proves a person's performance without producing harmful side effects.

_____   _____

22. Frustration occurs when individuals lack the ability to take necessary actions or when their actions are blocked by external obstacles.

_____   _____

23. Favorable life changes are never as stressful as unfavorable life changes.

_____   _____

24. The amount of stress individuals feel when in a crowd depends on how much control they think they have in the situation and on their cultural background.

_____   _____

25. An individual's reaction to stressors is determined by that person's prior attitudes, experiences, values, and even religion.

_____   _____

26. Thinking of oneself as helpless and worthless can lead to increased stress.

_____   _____

27. An individual's expectation about a stressful event can influence the individual's stress level significantly.

_____   _____

28. Physiological responses to stressors occur automati-

cally, without very much
conscious thought.   _____   _____

29. Hormones released under
     stress remain in the body
     for only a short period of
     time.   _____   _____

30. Arthritis and cancer may
     be indirectly related to
     stress.   _____   _____

31. A person under stress
     doesn't usually return to
     old habits if they're inap-
     propriate to the present
     situation.   _____   _____

32. An individual's stress level
     can increase if that indi-
     vidual receives no infor-
     mation or false informa-
     tion about a potentially
     stressful event prior to its
     occurrence.   _____   _____

33. During prolonged stress,
     the body enters a phase in
     which everything returns
     to a normal level of func-
     tioning without any
     symptom of stress.   _____   _____

34. Mental health problems,
     such as depression, should
     never be treated as emo-
     tional stress responses.   _____   _____

35. There is no evidence that
     stress causes an acceler-
     ation of the aging process.   _____   _____

36. Many cases of sexual dys-
    function, such as impo-
    tence, frigidity, and pre-
    mature ejaculation are a
    direct result of stress.   _____   _____

37. The body can be condi-
    tioned to relax just as
    quickly and easily as it's
    conditioned to tense up
    during stress.   _____   _____

38. One of the biggest sources
    of stress is the inability to
    make use of time.   _____   _____

39. Diet and nutrition are not
    very important factors in
    stress reactions.   _____   _____

40. Muscles that are con-
    stantly contracted lead to
    increased anxiety and
    emotional stress.   _____   _____

Scoring Key:
(1) T   (2) F   (3) T   (4) F   (5) F   (6) T   (7) F
(8) T   (9) T   (10) T   (11) F   (12) T   (13) T   (14) F
(15) F   (16) T   (17) T   (18) F   (19) F   (20) T   (21) T
(22) T   (23) F   (24) T   (25) T   (26) T   (27) T   (28) T
(29) F   (30) T   (31) F   (32) T   (33) T   (34) F   (35) F
(36) T   (37) T   (38) T   (39) F   (40) T

Total Number Correct _____   35—40   = Excellent
                                       30—34   = Good
                                       25—29   = Fair
                                       Less than 25 = Poor

COPING WITH STRESS

	TRUE	FALSE
1. Imagining heaviness and warmth in one's body parts is an effective relaxation technique.	_____	_____
2. An individual should consume more caffeine during stressful times.	_____	_____
3. Competitive physical activity is an effective stress management strategy.	_____	_____
4. Involvement in the pleasure of physical activity leads to feelings of well-being.	_____	_____
5. Breaking down complicated tasks into smaller parts can reduce stress.	_____	_____
6. Stress can be reduced by avoiding routines whenever possible.	_____	_____
7. When undergoing important life changes, stress can be reduced by increasing the number of other changes that are made.	_____	_____
8. Heartbeat can be monitored through biofeedback.	_____	_____
9. Individuals should not try to change their relation to stressors.	_____	_____

10. Sitting comfortably helps
     to quiet one's internal en-
     vironment.   _____   _____

11. Progressive muscle relax-
     ation is an effective tech-
     nique for relieving such
     illnesses as hypertension
     and ulcers.   _____   _____

12. Anticipating periods of
     boredom and planning ac-
     tivities for those periods
     can reduce stress.   _____   _____

13. When using physical exer-
     cise as a stress manage-
     ment technique, one
     should try to exert oneself
     as much as possible.   _____   _____

14. In muscle relaxation exer-
     cises, an individual at-
     tempts to eliminate the
     physical sensations that
     are associated with relax-
     ation.   _____   _____

15. Becoming less competitive
     with oneself and others is
     an effective way to reduce
     Type A behavior.   _____   _____

16. Delegating authority and
     responsibility to others
     will have no effect on
     stress.   _____   _____

17. To be effective, relaxation
     must be used at the same
     time and place each time
     it's done.   _____   _____

18. Being in a place away from other people helps to quiet one's internal environment.   _____   _____

19. Focusing on one's positive characteristics improves a person's self-image and reduces stress.   _____   _____

20. Increased muscle activity is a characteristic of relaxation.   _____   _____

21. Individuals shouldn't try to identify the environmental situations that prompt their stress.   _____   _____

22. Even if individuals can't change the nature of stressors, they can change their relation to stressors.   _____   _____

23. An effective way to reduce stress is to find alternatives for goals and behaviors that one has been unable to accomplish.   _____   _____

24. Listing tasks in order of their importance so that the most important tasks can be completed first helps to reduce stress.   _____   _____

25. Accepting the fact that no one can do everything perfectly helps to reduce stress.   _____   _____

26. Vacations, even when they

involve changes in loca-
tion, routine, or level of
stimulation, are always a
good way to relieve stress.   _____   _____

27. Effective relaxation can be
     achieved only when
     used regularly and in long
     spurts.   _____   _____

28. Physical activity that is
     vigorous enough to bring
     relaxation afterwards
     makes a person less open
     to the negative effects of
     stress.   _____   _____

29. People should learn ex-
     actly what types of situa-
     tions cause them to feel
     stress.   _____   _____

30. During relaxation, it's im-
     possible to feel nervous or
     anxious.   _____   _____

31. Relaxation happens when
     a person lets it happen in-
     stead of forcing it to
     happen.   _____   _____

32. Stress cannot be reduced
     by anticipating periods of
     boredom and planning
     something stimulating to
     do during those periods.   _____   _____

33. Stress cannot be reduced
     by establishing routines
     which become automatic.   _____   _____

34. Intentionally changing the

stressful aspects of one's
personality can help one
cope with many kinds of
stressors.   _____   _____

35. Developing close friend-
     ships with people one can
     trust reduces stress.   _____   _____

36. One of the best ways to re-
     duce emotional stress is
     through social support
     networks.   _____   _____

37. Older people can reduce
     stress by owning a pet.   _____   _____

38. Relaxation training allows
     people to regulate bodily
     processes that they
     thought were beyond con-
     scious control.   _____   _____

39. People who have difficult
     things to do increase their
     stress by setting time
     aside for breaks.   _____   _____

40. Sometimes the best way
     for individuals to decrease
     their stress is to avoid
     places or situations where
     they feel stress.   _____   _____

Scoring Key:
(1) T   (2) F   (3) F   (4) T   (5) T   (6) F   (7) F
(8) T   (9) F   (10) T (11) T (12) T (13) F (14) F
(15) T (16) F (17) F (18) T (19) T (20) F (21) F
(22) T (23) T (24) T (25) T (26) F (27) F (28) T
(29) T (30) T (31) T (32) F (33) F (34) T (35) T
(36) T (37) T (38) T (39) F (40) T

Total Number Correct _____   35—40   = Excellent
                                   30—34   = Good
                                   25—29   = Fair
                                   Less than 25 = Poor

RESPONSES TO STRESS

1. Valerie has just been promoted to a new job in a different city. An appropriate way for Valerie to reduce her stress would be:

   A. Change her hairstyle and way of dressing to reflect her new image.

   B. Take on as much work as she can to keep herself busy.

   C. Establish a suitable schedule soon after she arrives.

   D. Avoid responsibility as much as possible at first.

2. John is in a noisy office and is trying to concentrate on his work. An appropriate way for John to reduce his stress would be to:

   A. Skip lunch and work during lunch hour when the office is quieter.

   B. Rearrange the books and papers on his desk.

   C. Wear more comfortable clothes to work.

   D. Take periodic breaks away from the office to get some relief.

3. David is worried that he will fail his history test, even though he has studied hard for it. An appropriate way for David to reduce his stress would be to:

   A. Stay up late the night before the test in order to study more.

   B. Think about how angry his parents will be if he fails the test.

   C. Go out and take a bicycle ride.

   D. Get up early the next morning and study some more.

4. Arthur is very busy typing when a co-worker asks him to help her with her typing. An appropriate way for Arthur to reduce his stress would be to:

   A. Help her with her typing but explain that he won't do it again.

B. Explain that he can't do her typing and concentrate on finishing his own work.

C. Pretend that his co-worker's request doesn't bother him and continue working.

D. Tell his co-worker that he'll do her typing after he's finished with his.

5. David has been told that there is no chance that he can pitch for his baseball team because the manager's brother will be taking his place. An appropriate way for David to reduce his stress would be to:

A. Look into pitching for another team.

B. Get to know the other members of the team better.

C. Tell the owner that he insists on being able to pitch for the team, no matter what.

D. Quit pitching altogether.

6. Kathy drives home on a busy, crowded freeway. An appropriate way for Kathy to reduce her stress would be to:

A. Drive with the car windows open slightly.

B. Make sure that she takes the same route home whenever possible.

C. Drink a cup of coffee as she drives.

D. Try an alternate route or a different time when it's not as crowded.

7. Gary is concerned that the quality of his work is not good enough, even though all of the people he works with tell him he's doing a good job. An appropriate way for Gary to reduce his stress would be to:

A. Spend more time working to improve the quality of his work.

B. Plan to have a few beers with his co-workers every day after work.

C. Spend more time focusing on the positive qualities of his work.

D. Look for another line of work that would make him more satisfied.

8. Leslie has just recently married and moved to a new city. An appropriate way for Leslie to reduce her stress would be to:

   A. Try to change her old habits.

   B. Set aside some time each day to relax.

   C. Take a vacation with her husband.

   D. Take on extra work to keep her mind busy.

9. Sharon works on an assembly line where she watches metal fittings go by all day long. An appropriate way for Sharon to reduce her stress would be to:

   A. Bring in a soft cushion for her chair.

   B. Ask her boss if she can listen to a radio as she works.

   C. See if she can work through lunch so that she can finish her work as quickly as possible.

   D. Increase her work load to keep her mind occupied.

10. Karen had been planning on taking a week off from work. Now her boss tells Karen that it's impossible for her to have the vacation time she had planned. An appropriate way for Karen to reduce her stress would be to:

    A. Threaten to switch jobs unless she can take her vacation as planned.

    B. Act as if she didn't want the time off that much anyway.

    C. Tell her boss that she's disappointed and ask if she can take the time off next month.

    D. Act angry enough to convince her boss to give her the time off she wanted.

11. Jennifer has four final exams and only two days left to study for them. An appropriate way for Jennifer to reduce her stress would be to:

    A. Take her mind off her own tests by helping a friend study.

B. Pick the hardest course and study for that exam only.

C. Study for each of her tests, one at a time.

D. Try to spend twice as much time as she usually does studying for the exams.

12. Gwen wants to be president of a local club but has been told that she lacks the organization ability. An appropriate way for Gwen to reduce her stress would be to:

A. Stop attending club meetings.

B. Take a business class to improve her skills.

C. Tell the club members that she doesn't really want to be the president.

D. Accept the fact that she can never be the president.

13. Gregg lives across from an all night gas station and is disturbed by the noise from the cars. An appropriate way for Gregg to reduce his stress would be to:

A. Play loud music to block out the noise.

B. Take a sleeping pill to help get to sleep.

C. Give all of his business to another gas station.

D. Use relaxation techniques to help block out noise.

14. Stanley is surrounded by people at a very crowded party. An appropriate way for Stanley to reduce his stress would be to:

A. Stay in the middle of the crowd.

B. Have several extra glasses of wine in order to relax.

C. Loosen his tie so that he will feel more comfortable.

D. Get away from the crowd and stay in an area that's more comfortable for him.

15. Joyce must speak to a large group of people and keeps thinking about the time she was giving a speech in front of her class and forgot what she was to say. An appropriate way for Joyce to reduce her stress would be to:

A. Set aside some time before the speech to relax.

B. Remember as many details as she can about her previous experience giving a speech.

C. Keep her hands busy while she gives the speech.

D. Review her speech until the last minute in order to be better prepared.

Scoring Key:
The responses to the preceding questions fall into one of five response categories. They are:

Appropriate	a response that is correct or appropriate for the situation.
Unhealthy	a response that is unhealthy.
Violation	a response that is in direct violation of the appropriate responses to stress.
Denial	a response that denies the stress or the problem producing the stress.
Ineffective	a response that is related to the situation but is ineffective in reducing stress. It is neither unhealthy, nor in direct violation, nor a denial.

No.	Appropriate	Unhealthy	Violation	Denial	Ineffective
1.	C	—	A	D	B
2.	D	A	—	—	B,C
3.	C	A	B,D	—	—
4.	B	—	A	C	D
5.	A	—	C	—	B,D
6.	D	C	—	—	A,B
7.	C	B	—	—	A,D
8.	B	—	A,C	—	D
9.	B	C	D	—	A
10.	C	—	A,D	B	—
11.	C	—	A,D	—	B
12.	B	—	—	C	A,D
13.	D	B	A	—	C
14.	D	B	A	—	C
15.	A	—	B,D	—	C

STRESS SOURCE AND RESISTANCE SURVEY

The following survey describes various conditions or times when people might feel stress. Read each statement and circle YES or NO to show if you would feel stress at that time. Each time you circle YES, place a number from 0 to 10 to show how certain you are that you could manage the stress from that situation. The 0 to 10 scale corresponds to the following certainty limits:

0	1	2	3	4	5	6	7	8	9	10
Very Uncertain				Somewhat Certain				Very Certain		

Situation	Might you feel stress?	If Yes, how certain are you that you could manage the stress?
1. You're trying to concentrate but you're constantly being interrupted.	YES/NO	____
2. You have to do a very boring task.	YES/NO	____
3. You've been thinking about someone who hurt you in the past.	YES/NO	____
4. You have a neighbor who plays loud music all the time.	YES/NO	____
5. You have several things to finish in a very short time.	YES/NO	____

6. You're home by yourself
    and feel lonely.   YES/NO   ____

7. You're in a crowded bus
    and can't get to the exit in
    time for your stop.   YES/NO   ____

8. You keep thinking about
    an unpleasant experience.   YES/NO   ____

9. You've taken on more than
    you can do.   YES/NO   ____

10. You're waiting on the
    street for someone to pick
    you up, and you're getting
    cold.   YES/NO   ____

11. Although you have plenty
    of time, you're worried
    you'll be late for an impor-
    tant appointment.   YES/NO   ____

12. Your closest friend has left
    town and you feel alone.   YES/NO   ____

13. You're in a room that's ex-
    tremely hot.   YES/NO   ____

14. You must buy a gift for
    someone and the stores
    are closing.   YES/NO   ____

15. You saw someone being
    robbed and keep imagin-
    ing that it could happen to
    you.   YES/NO   ____

16. You have to wait for a de-
    livery and you have noth-
    ing to do.   YES/NO   ____

17. Your friends keep asking
you to do things you don't
want to do.   YES/NO   ____

18. You must get a prescrip-
tion filled and you can't
find a drug store that's
open.   YES/NO   ____

19. You spend a good deal of
time in a place that's very
noisy.   YES/NO   ____

20. No matter how hard
you've tried, you haven't
been able to finish all your
work.   YES/NO   ____

Scoring

1. Add all the numerical certainty scores   ____

2. Count all the "YES" responses   ____

3. Count all the "NO" responses   ____

4. Divide No. 2 by No. 1   ____

5. Add No. 3 to No. 4. for a final score of   ____

17–20 = Excellent stress resistance and management ability.

13–16 = Good stress resistance and good management ability.

10–12 = Fair stress resistance and management ability.

0–9   = Poor stress resistance and management ability.

This survey also can be used to indicate the number and
types of stress situations in which you feel pressure. Count the
number of "YES" responses. The maximum score of 20 indi-

cates that you feel stress in all specified situations. The minimum score of 0 indicates that you feel stress in none of the specified situations.

In addition to an overall score, your responses also can be linked to specific stress sources. To determine the kinds of stresses you're susceptible to, compare the situations to which you responded YES and scored poorly on to the sources of stress below.

SOURCE OF STRESS	SITUATIONS			
Physical stress	4,	10,	13,	19
Frustration	1,	7,	14,	18
Emotional Stress	3,	8,	11,	15
Poor time management	5,	9,	17,	20
Deprivation	2,	6,	12,	16

STRESS MANAGEMENT
SURVEY

This survey describes things that people might do to manage stress. Read each statement and circle YES or NO to show if you intend to do what's described in the item. Each time you circle YES, place a number from 0 to 10 to show how strong your intention is. The 0 to 10 scale corresponds to the following intention limits.

1 Very Weak	2	3	4	5	6	7	8	9	10 Very Strong

	Do you intend to do this?	If YES, how strong is your intention?
1. Find alternatives for goals you've been unable to reach.	YES/NO	_____
2. Stay away from crowded places if they make you feel nervous.	YES/NO	_____
3. Do the most important things first when you have too many things to do.	YES/NO	_____
4. Find interesting things to do when you're bored.	YES/NO	_____
5. Use earplugs when you're in noisy places.	YES/NO	_____
6. Avoid unnecessary changes when you have many other things to do.	YES/NO	_____

7. Look at the positive things in yourself and your life. YES/NO ____

8. Take one thing at a time. YES/NO ____

9. Get plenty of sleep every night. YES/NO ____

10. Talk about your problems with friends and family. YES/NO ____

11. Talk about your problems with the people who are involved with them. YES/NO ____

12. Balance work with relaxing activities. YES/NO ____

13. Use relaxation techniques. YES/NO ____

14. Get regular exercise. YES/NO ____

15. Avoid large amounts of caffeine. YES/NO ____

16. Try to identify what's causing you stress. YES/NO ____

17. Accept realistic goals for yourself and others. YES/NO ____

18. Avoid having many big changes come at the same time. YES/NO ____

19. Get professional help if you feel too much stress. YES/NO ____

20. Accept what you cannot change. YES/NO ____

Scoring

This survey can be scored in two ways, as follows:

A. Count the number of "YES" responses, disregarding the numerical intention scores. The maximum score of 20 means that you have a strong intention to use a variety of stress management techniques. A score of less than 15 indicates that you may or may not intend to utilize stress management in certain situations. You should evaluate the "NO" responses and determine why you can't.

B. Add all the numerical intention scores that correspond to the "YES" responses and divide the total number by 20 (the total number of items in the survey). The maximum score of 10 indicates a very strong intention to use stress management techniques. A score of 6 or less indicates that you have some work to do on specific areas of stress management and need to reevaluate how important it is for you to manage the stress in your life.

Appendix

SOCIAL SUPPORT
MUTUAL HELP GROUPS

Social support networks and mutual help groups can be one of the best ways of coping with various negative life experiences. The following is a listing of some of the most common support and mutual help groups. Many of these groups publish newsletters and information pamphlets and have local offices. Write to them and ask for information about their organization, or contact your doctor for advice.

UNITED KINGDOM

Alcoholism

ALCOHOLICS ANONYMOUS, P.O. Box 1, Stonebow House, Stonebow, York, North Yorkshire, YO1 2NJ

ACCEPT SERVICES (Drinkwatchers), 724 Fulham Road, London, SW6 5SE

Bereavement

CRUISE, Cruise House, 126 Sheen Road, Richmond, Surrey, TW9 1UR

COMPASSIONATE FRIENDS (bereaved parents), 53 North Street, Bristol, Avon, BS3 1EN

Counselling

SAMARITANS, (please consult your local telephone directory for your nearest branch)

Depression

DEPRESSIVES ANONYMOUS, 36 Chestnut Avenue, Beverley, North Humberside, HU17 9QU

Divorce

DIVORCE CONCILIATION AND ADVISORY SERVICE, 38 Ebury Street, London, SW1 0LU

Gambling

GAMBLERS ANONYMOUS, P.O. Box 88, London, SW10 0EU

Loneliness

NEXUS, Nexus House, 6 The Quay, Bideford, North Devon, EX39 2HW

Marriage Guidance

RELATE, Herbert Gray College, Little Church Street, Rugby, Warwickshire, CV21 3AP

One Parent Families

GINGERBREAD, 35 Wellington Street, London, WC2E 7BN

Retirement

ASSOCIATION OF RETIRED PERSONS, Greencoat House, Francis Street, London, SW1 1DZ

Victim Support

VICTIM SUPPORT, Cramner House, 39 Brixton Road, London, SW9 6DZ

AUSTRALIA

Alcoholism

ALCOHOLICS ANONYMOUS, 127 Edwin Street, Croydon, Sydney 2132, NSW

Bereavement

NATIONAL ASSOCIATION FOR LOSS AND GRIEF, P.O. Box 79, Bobbin Heads 2074, NSW

Depression

MENTAL HEALTH INFORMATION REFERRAL SERVICE, 62 Victoria Road, Gladesville 2111, NSW

Divorce and Marriage Guidance

MARRIAGE GUIDANCE, 5 Sera Street, Lane Cove 2066, NSW

Gambling

GAMBLERS ANONYMOUS, P.O. Box 142, Burwood 2134, NSW

Incest

INCEST SURVIVORS ASSOCIATION, 88 Edward Street, East Perth 6000, WA

Loneliness

LIFELINE, 148 Lonsdale Street, Melbourne 3000, Victoria

One Parent Families

PARENTS WITHOUT PARTNERS, 19 Clarence Street,
South Brisbane 4104, Queensland

Retirement

AUSTRALIAN RETIRED PERSONS ASSOCIATION, 9th
Floor, 150 Queen Street, Melbourne 3000, Victoria

Victim Support

VICTIMS OF CRIME ASSISTANCE LEAGUE, 71 Eastern
Road, South Melbourne 3205, Victoria

NEW ZEALAND

Alcoholism

ALCOHOLICS ANONYMOUS, P.O. Box 458, Wellington,

Divorce and Marriage Guidance

THE BEGINNING EXPERIENCE, Pompalier Diocesan Centre, Private Bag 47 904, Auckland

Gambling

COMPULSIVE GAMBLING SOCIETY OF NEW ZEALAND, P.O. 37 438, Auckland

Incest

HOME AND FAMILY SOCIETY, 344 Mount Eden Road, Mount Eden, Auckland

Marriage Guidance

MARRIAGE GUIDANCE NEW ZEALAND, P.O. Box 2729, Wellington

Retirement

AGE CONCERN, 150 Featherston Street, Wellington

Victim Support

NEW ZEALAND COUNCIL OF VICTIM SUPPORT GROUPS, P.O. Box 3017, Wellington

Widowed Persons

WIDOWS' AND WIDOWERS' ASSOCIATION OF NEW
ZEALAND, P.O. Box 11 595, Wellington

SOUTH AFRICA

Alcoholism

ALCOHOLICS ANONYMOUS, Box 7228, Johannesburg 2000

ALCOHOLICS ANONYMOUS INFORMATION SERVICES FOR FAMILIES OF ALCOHOLICS, Delbree House, Bree Street, Johannesburg 2000

Depression

NATIONAL COUNCIL FOR MENTAL HEALTH, P.O. Box 2587, Johannesburg 2000

Divorce and Marriage Guidance

DIVORCE COUNSELLING, Old Arcade, Market Street, Johannesburg 2000

Family Advice and Therapy

FAMILY AND MARRIAGE SOCIETY OF SOUTH AFRICA, P.O. Box 2800, Kempton Park 1620

FAMILY LIFE CENTRE, 1 Parkwood, Cardigan Road, Johannesburg 2000

CHILD WELFARE SOCIETY, Box 2539, Johannesburg 2000

Loneliness

SUICIDE PREVENTION CENTRE / SUICIDE ANONY-MOUS, Box 9837, Johannesburg 2000

Retirement and Age Concern

NATIONAL COUNCIL FOR THE AGED, P.O. Box 2335, Cape Town 8000

Victim Support

LIFE LINE, Box 95135, Grant Park 2051